UNLEASH THE STORRIE™ WITHIN

COMPILED BY
DR. CHRISTINE MANUKYAN

No part of this publication may be reproduced, stored in a retrieval system, or transmitted in any form or by any means—electronic, photocopying, recording, or otherwise—without prior written permission, except in the case of brief excerpts in critical reviews and articles. For permission requests, contact Dr. Christine Manukyan at drchristine@storrie.co

All rights reserved.

Published by STORRIE™ Publishing

Copyright © 2021 Dr. Christine Manukyan

Editing and Copy by Gary and Danielle Damrell

Cover Design by Jennifer Rae

ISBN: 9798495469471

The author disclaims responsibility for adverse effects or consequences from the misapplication or injudicious use of the information contained in this book. Mention of resources and associations does not imply an endorsement.

*To those who have felt stuck, undervalued,
and overworked yet continue to overcome:
You are seen, heard, and needed. Your work is not in vain.*

*To those who have dedicated their lives to the healthcare industry:
Thank you for standing on the front lines during unprecedented times,
we honor you. You are saving lives.*

*Keep walking forward and soon you will discover the path towards
unleashing your own STORRIE™ that already exists within you.*

*We all deserve a second chance to rewrite our STORRIE™
and become the best version of ourselves.*

TABLE OF CONTENTS

About the Authors 1

Foreword 5

Chapter 1. Leading the Functional Medicine Revolution 9
By: Christine Manukyan, PharmD, MS

Chapter 2. The Path Towards Healing and Empowerment 29
By: Allie Burch MSN, FNP-C, MCN, IFMCP

Chapter 3. Turning Down the White Noise 43
By: Angela S. Garcia, PharmD, MPH, CPh

Chapter 4. Born For Something More 65
By: Ani Rostomyan, PharmD, BCPS, APh

Chapter 5. From Unheard Struggles to Reclaiming Freedom: A Mom's Journey to Real Answers 81
By: Areeman Saed, PharmD

Chapter 6. A New Perspective Yields Hope for Change 95
By: Brooke Spino, PharmD

Chapter 7. There Is a Better Way! 109
By: Emily Saparito, PharmD

Chapter 8. Failure Is Not a Trait, But Rather, a Temporary Event 121
By: Gaby Udabor, FNP-C

Chapter 9. The Power of Self-Healing Comes from Within .. 133
By: Hona Kandi, ND, MBA

Chapter 10. MNDSHFT for Elevated Health,
an Aligned Career, and a Vibrant Life 145
By: Jennifer Wheeler, MS, MSN, FMP, NP-C

Chapter 11. Beginning My Journey with
Functional Medicine 157
By: Kristina Telhami,
Doctor of Pharmacy Candidate (PharmD), 2022

Chapter 12. A Road to Ikigai 171
By: Krystyna Shepetiuk, PharmD, CDCES

Chapter 13. Living Life on Your Terms 187
By: Lisette Miranda Alba, PharmD, BS

Chapter 14. Taking Charge of Our Health 201
By: Marlene Nanda Rosana, FNP-C, DNP

Chapter 15. Uncovering My Why 213
By: Rajinder Rai, PharmD, FAAMFM

Chapter 16. Lighting the Path Towards Holistic Freedom 227
By: Rojan Ghorbannejad,
Doctor of Pharmacy Candidate (PharmD), 2022

Chapter 17. Changing Lives Without Medication 239
By: Svetlana Stepanskiy, PharmD

Chapter 18. Saying "Yes!" to Rewriting My Story 251
By: Tammy Lopez, PharmD, BC-ADM, CDCES

Chapter 19. From Darkness into the Light 267
By: Zsuzsanna Coniglio, PharmD

ABOUT THE AUTHORS
by Dr. Christine Manukyan

"If you can't, you must. If you must, you can."
– Tony Robbins

When you make the decision to stop allowing fear to get in your way, you unlock the potential to change your life, and the lives of those around you. When I left my job during the global pandemic in 2020 and started my entrepreneurial journey, I manifested that I would create a tribe of 20 badass women and visualized the ways our lives would change forever. I didn't know HOW, but I knew WHY having this tribe was important. Guess what? Today, that manifestation has come true, and these women have become authors, sharing their stories, and changing the world. These authors are RESILIENT, and you will be inspired so much. At the time that *Unleash the STORRIE Within*™ is being released, I am celebrating the one-year anniversary of launching the Functional Medicine Business Academy™. I am also excited to announce our new collaborative Functional Medicine Practice, *STORRIE Wellness*™, which is launching November 11th, 2021. 11-11 is a very special day and carries a lot of significance. 11-11 serves as a reminder to keep looking forward, accept the change that's coming, and step into the blessings and opportunities around you. The stories in this collaborative book serve as evidence that anyone can reclaim their power, unlock their impact, and unleash the STORRIE™ from within.

Being stuck is challenging. Not long ago, I was stuck in two separate worlds. I experienced an immense amount of emotional and mental stress during the pandemic, and it was one of my darkest moments in life. I was just like everyone else, a clinician who didn't really know what was possible. Through beginning to invest into my personal growth and learning from mentors like Tony Robbins, I began to develop the tools to discover how to turn my excuses into my WHY and rewrite my story. When I made the decision to leave my job on August 28, 2020, I took the entire month of September to slow down and manifest my dreams and desires. I knew I was meant to make an impact in this world, so it was time to make some drastic changes to alter the course of my life. I owed this to myself and to others. It was time. I am so grateful that I chose to walk away from fear to gain the freedom I've always longed for.

Originally, I left my job because I had no childcare, and I was tired of choosing between my family and my career. I just knew, deep inside me, I had a calling. I am to bring HOPE to other women and to lead them in changing lives and healing the world from within. I have gone all-in to create this legacy. They say, "If you build it, they will come." Brick by brick, I saw this to be true. And today I am excited to share with you, this special tribe that was born. My plan was to scale my Functional Medicine Practice, but instead, Functional Medicine Business Academy™ became my HOW to enter into my calling. When you pour your heart and soul into something, others notice.

These women have proven to be there for me from day one. Every one of these authors have impacted my life in so many ways I could never even begin to fully express. This tribe has kept me going, especially when times have been really hard. For example, these past few weeks were awful for our entire family, as we all had covid. Thankfully, because of this tribe and lifestyle we've built, I was able to take the time we've needed to rest and recover. I didn't have to beg my boss for days off or worry about not having enough vacation hours to cover my absence. Now, I am not stressed about reporting to someone and explaining why I need to be home. I have worked really hard to create financial freedom and time freedom. Life will always happen and it's always full of surprises, so why not do everything you can to make space for those surprises? I am excited to be a part of building lasting legacies for myself, this tribe, and beyond. I am excited to be a part of several growing businesses where surprises are accepted, honored, and supported. Through the support of my tribe and team, I was able to fully recover, without the fear of letting people down or failing as an employee. I was able to heal, rest, and focus on my family and health, while my legacy and business continued growing. Therefore, I chose to pursue this lifestyle. It wasn't easy, but it's so worth it.

These authors have become my best friends and sisters. We laugh together, we cry together, and we always have each other's back. Each woman came into my life, at this time, for a distinct reason. Individually, they have gone through a lot and until this moment, their stories have been locked away within them, just waiting to be honored and shared. This is one of the main goals of this book - To honor the stories shared, so that their legacies can live on and help YOU unleash your own truth and continue to spread healing and growth from within. They all bring in their unique voices and gifts into the Functional Medicine Business Academy™ and into the upcoming STORRIE Wellness™. This is my tribe, and together we **UNLEASH THE STORRIE™ WITHIN.**

FOREWORD

By Rebecca Cafiero

As a child, we're told we can do and be anything we want. Our life before us is an empty book, and it's our privilege to fill the pages with the story as we live it. We're starting a journey with endless possibilities and promises of adventure.

Yet we're greatly affected by the circumstances we grow up in, the conditioning from our parents and family, the teachers randomly assigned, the attitudes of our social circle, the expectations, and labels such as gender, color, nationality, and economic status that we have no control over coming into this world.

There's often an expected path revealed for us from these conditions, and "choice" is limited by opportunity, timing, and the sheer possibility we know to be available by our limited experience and circle of influence.

When we commit to a lofty endeavor or career, we invest our precious commodities of money and time into the goal, or time and emotion into a relationship. The path forward becomes narrower and more defined. Veering from it seems impulsive, reckless, and even selfish. The more of our story that's written, the more emotionally and logistically challenging to change the plot.

At some point, whether caused by age or a life shifting event, we stop to review the journey so far, and the path ahead. To really ask ourselves if the story we're writing is the stuff epic novels are constructed of or merely a mundane read we can't muster our way through. If we're not happy with it, we have two choices. Either to take radical responsibility for our results and make the changes necessary to live a life we love that we can be proud of, or to change nothing, but end up dissatisfied, depressed or living in regret.

When diagnosed with cancer or other serious illnesses, or after great loss, people seem to make drastic life changes. But really, they gain a new perspective, an awareness of the limited time we have and take a look to see if the path they're on is worth staying on. The inner voice, that started as a whisper, gets louder, asking for what the heart really wants. And the reasons to stay on the path, the time and money invested, the expectations of others that don't guarantee our own happiness, seem quieter, less important.

The realization that working to make others happy will never ensure our own happiness, and rarely, our legacy, becomes apparent. And that is when inspired change happens. That is when our real path is found, and our story becomes legendary.

The incredible individuals whose stories make up Unleash Your Storrie Within, all who dedicated their life to helping their fellow humans, had the courage to listen to that inner voice. They've taken the risk to change their direction and pursue the magical destination where purpose and happiness merge. These are their stories.

ABOUT REBECCA CAFIERO

Rebecca Cafiero is an international Forbes Business & PR strategist, TEDx Speaker and top ranked podcast host, 2x best-selling author and mother of two.

As the Founder and CEO of the Pitch Club, a for women, by women company, she has worked with hundreds of female entrepreneurs to increase their credibility, visibility and profitability in business. Her clients have been featured in countless publications, from magazines including Forbes, the Wall Street Journal, Entrepreneur Magazine and Martha Stewart to popular digital publications such as Authority Magazine, Birdie, Medium and Buzzfeed.

Her publishing house, Pitch Club Publishing, has co-created 19 female best-selling authors and counting. Podcast Camp, a podcast creation and launch program, has helped launch more than a dozen top ranked, New and Noteworthy podcasts with hundreds of thousands of downloads.

Prior to becoming an entrepreneur, she spent 13 years in Corporate America leading sales and marketing teams. She is a frequent speaker on online business strategy, creating credibility + visibility, productivity, and personal optimization. As a sought-after media source, Rebecca's tips have been featured in NBC News, ABC News, BIZ TV and publications including Forbes, Reader's Digest, Women's Health, US News and World Report and more. She' s passionate about educating and empowering female entrepreneurs to be seen, heard and valued as an expert in their field.

Chapter 1

LEADING THE FUNCTIONAL MEDICINE REVOLUTION

By Christine Manukyan, PharmD, MS

> *"The doctor of the future will give no medication but will instruct his patients in the care of the human frame, diet and in the cause and prevention of disease."*
>
> – THOMAS EDISON

I have never been fired from a job, but I fired my boss during a global pandemic in order to create my own functional medicine legacy. In September 2020, an eye-opening 865,000 women left the U.S. workforce. Research shows that this is four times more women than men in 2020 alone. I was one of those women. For my 40th birthday I became a corporate dropout because I was exhausted from the demands of childcare, homeschooling, housework and having a full-time job on the front lines as a healthcare provider. I made the decision to put my family first and chose holistic preventative healthcare over traditional medicine.

This decision to pivot in my career was extremely challenging. In Aug 2020, however, I left my secure hospital job and exactly a year later, I am celebrating a 6-figure month in the realm of entrepreneurship while making the real impact I have always dreamed of. I was done with making excuses and waiting for the "right time." Now is the only right time, so I stepped out of my own way and got to work. In just over a year, I created my own virtual functional medicine practice, launched the Functional Medicine Business Academy™, launched the STORRIE™ Podcast and wrote a best-selling book, *Pivot with Purpose*. All of these decisions took a lot of dedication, grit, and commitment, but I am determined to rewrite my STORRIE™ and help others create their own functional medicine legacy.

You may be asking, "How did someone like me who has been a hospital clinical pharmacist for 13 years accomplish all these unconventional tasks so quickly?" The truth is, I did not go to school for business, I had no experience with entrepreneurship, nor did I attend school for functional medicine. Nevertheless, my life and experiences have prepared me for this very moment. My own health transformation journey opened endless opportunities to rewrite my story, learn and teach about functional medicine, and begin my entrepreneurial voyage. I finally have the opportunity to dream again, live my life with intention and purpose, and help other practitioners to do the same. This is the beginning of the functional medicine uprising the pharmaceutical industry has needed for far too long.

At 16 years old, I moved to the United States and became a first generation Armenian American. One of the first things I had to get used to was the "American diet." I didn't know about things like processed food, GMO, artificial colors and sweeteners, chemicals, preservatives, pesticides, and I could go on and on. I grew up watching my grandparents use home remedies whenever we caught a cold or flu, and we rarely used any medications to treat anything. Growing up I only knew about organic food because back home, during the 80s, that's all we had. Organic fresh food was our nutrition and our medicine. I grew up drinking water from the water faucet without thinking twice about if it had any additional chemicals. I grew up eating butter every day without worrying about cholesterol. We walked everywhere, occasionally taking public transportation, but I was constantly active and moving my body. We shopped at farmer's markets and ate fruits and vegetables that were in season. Looking back, I wondered if we lived in a bubble or did we grow up with an ideal healthy lifestyle that was easy to take for granted. I wasn't sure what the answer was, and the more crappy and cheap fast food I consumed as a teenager, the more I realized how sick my body was becoming. I found myself gaining weight, I was struggling with energy, and I was having a hard time focusing. This was not normal for me. Ultimately, my diet and lifestyle were affecting my mood, self-esteem and worth. My family couldn't afford to purchase organic food, as we were living paycheck to paycheck and received government assistance at the time. We could only afford cheap fast food that had absolutely no nutritional value and was just filled with crap.

If you grew up in the United States, my story may not resonate with you, as you may only know this American lifestyle as your norm. However, as someone who was new to this environment, I had no idea of the long-term health issues this traditional "American diet" can cause. Growing up as a teenager and trying to just fit in, I acclimated to this new lifestyle and little did I know, this would be the beginning of my health challenges that caught up with me once I entered my 30s. The bad eating and exercise habits continued through my time in undergraduate and pharmacy school. I remember drinking 3 to 4 cans of diet soda each day, adding 5 to 7 packets of Splenda into my coffee, and eating ramen noodles filled with soy, sodium, and GMOs. I thought to myself, "I am young, I don't have any health issues, so why not?" And when you add stress on top of a poor lifestyle, you may not know it, but you are slowly dying inside.

Like many others, I was trading my health for potential wealth and was focused on achieving the "American dream." I worked hard throughout pharmacy school and graduated with honors while being class president, and president of several organizations. I was also working part-time at a retail pharmacy, and to be honest, it was rough. After graduating from Nova Southeastern University College of Pharmacy, I was chasing after the next big thing. This meant moving to Ohio from Florida and living alone for the first time while completing a 2-year residency at The Ohio State University Medical Center while working on my master's degree in Health-System Pharmacy Administration.

Before I knew it, I found myself stuck and again telling myself, "I am young, it's ok, one day I'll get back on track." Within weeks after graduating from my residency, I got married to my high school sweetheart, who also happened to become a hospital pharmacist. We quickly started expanding our family and began having children. Having back-to-back pregnancies, and working full time at the hospital, took a huge toll on my health. Chasing after promotions and living my life on autopilot as a newlywed with two little ones at home with no childcare took a huge toll on my health. While I was climbing the leadership ladder at work, I was slowly dying inside. Plus, back-to-back pregnancies caused more weight gain and my health spiraled out of control. As a new mother, I was focused on my family, work, and others, and forgot all about self-love and self-care. I became morbidly obese and saw my health declining as my career was seemingly blooming. My energy was almost nonexistent, and I was unable to be fully present with my kids.

In 2015, at age 35, I scheduled my annual checkup. At this appointment, I was told by my primary care physician that I was going to have a heart attack in the next 5 years if I continued with the lifestyle I had been living. I mean, who wants to hear they are going to die at age 40? That was scary, but the truth was, I was morbidly obese, extremely burnt out, had high cholesterol, low energy, insomnia, brain fog, unexplained inflammation, and high stress. I can honestly say I was a hot mess mamma living on autopilot, trying to take care of my two little ones while also working full time as a hospital pharmacist in various leadership roles. From the outside, I looked fine, and I wasn't "sick." It was only my cholesterol that was high, all the other lab tests came back perfect. During that office visit, I was given a pill to lower my cholesterol and I was told to lose weight. I wasn't given any guidance on how to go about losing weight or what other options I had. I was just given a toxic pill with many side effects. It was stunning and left me feeling humiliated. I blamed myself and kept thinking, "I should have known better." I felt confused and as if I had lost part of my identity. I knew I had to make changes, but I had no clue where to start.

I walked out of that 10-minute doctor's appointment, that I waited 6 months to get scheduled, and waited over an hour before I was seen by the doctor. After the appointment, I sat in my car crying and began to feel increasingly more anxious about how I was going to fix this. I was overwhelmed and terrified at the thought of not being around to watch my children grow. I just knew there had to be a better way to reclaim my health and life without pharmaceuticals.

This appointment had me spinning. I wanted to know why, as a patient, I was left to feel this way. Why wasn't my doctor asking me how I feel about taking a pill or even having a conversation about what else we could do before I start taking prescription medications to lower my cholesterol? Why isn't my doctor even asking me how I am? If I was asked how I was really feeling, I would have shared that I was going through my very first burnout, I was not fine, and I was not OK. The reality is routine labs don't always tell the story of how a person is feeling. They just don't.

Without even realizing it, I had been sitting in my car for over an hour thinking about what just happened. I had to gather my strength and pull myself together so I could drive home and face the reality that I wasn't prepared to face. As I was driving, I kept praying and manifesting for someone to come into my life who could help me. I needed someone who could be my accountability buddy to help me lose weight without starving myself. I had failed so many diets in the past that I was tired of unsuccessful dieting attempts that led me nowhere near being "healthy." I knew a decision needed to be made, so I started researching and gave myself time to discover a better way to lower my cholesterol and lose some weight.

"It is in your moments of decision that your destiny is shaped."
— Tony Robbins.

I knew I had to make a decision that would change my life forever. Either I had to settle and just take the pill, or I could challenge myself to look for an alternative. Spoiler alert, I chose option two. I focused my energy on looking for alternative ways to heal my body. Taking care of my health suddenly became my top priority. After several weeks of searching, I found a solution. My friend and colleague introduced me to holistic health, and that led me to the best Mother's Day present I could have ever given myself. On Mother's Day in 2015, I committed to rewriting my story in order to become the best version of myself. This commitment led me towards learning about functional medicine, and I began focusing more on the root cause of my failing health and relearning how to use food as medicine. I also realized my health was connected to my highly stressful career, so I made the decision to step down from my current management position to work as a clinical staff pharmacist in hopes of bringing down my stress levels. This was a very hard decision to make, especially since this was the first time after all these years, I was no longer the "boss." It was time for something to change and I had to focus on what mattered the most to me, which was my health and my family. Putting aside my ego and title to focus on a healthy lifestyle was incredibly challenging, but it was one of the best decisions I have ever made. For the first time in my life, I had to really ask myself, "How am I really doing?" Being "fine" or just "OK" was not good enough for me. I needed time to go back to the basics. For 16 years I lived an unhealthy lifestyle, and I was over it.

Six months after my last doctor's appointment, I went in for a follow-up. My doctor wanted to make sure my labs were OK, as I was supposed to start taking the cholesterol lowering medication. I intentionally didn't say anything about not taking the medication, as I wanted to share what else I was doing during the time. I had started making holistic lifestyle changes. I can remember this moment so clearly. My doctor walked in the room and told me, "I think there is a lab error. We might have to redo your labs. Your labs are normal, and I don't think the medication works that fast." I smiled at her and told her that there is no lab error. What she was looking at was the power of using food as medicine, incorporating adaptogens for stress management and natural energy, cellular cleansing, and intermittent fasting. I had lost 35 pounds of toxic visceral fat, the fat that was surrounding my organs and causing all the health issues I was experiencing. When I started to share with her what I was doing for the last 6 months, she was so impressed and asked me to send her information so she could share it with her other patients. She even asked me if I was OK with her connecting me with others who would like to learn more about my lifestyle. I got the green light to continue what I was doing and not stop. That one decision to change my health without pharmaceuticals and instead incorporate functional medicine, became the catalyst of my life transformation journey, that later on became my career as a Functional Medicine Practitioner.

After experiencing my own health transformation using functional medicine, I realized the power of making decisions and how one decision can transform your entire life. Over time, I went on to lose over 100 pounds through intermittent fasting, exercise, and incorporating functional medicine practices into my daily routine. I even experienced a boost of self-confidence that allowed me to step out onstage as a fitness competitor (bodybuilder)— a real-life Wonder Woman—in order to empower other women to say "Yes!" to themselves, and to provide an example of what's possible when you take consistent action every single day. As a matter of fact, I ran the LA Marathon on March 8, 2020, for my 40th birthday! Mamma didn't have a heart attack like the doctor said. Instead, she ran a marathon that took her 9 months of training and 5:58:04 to cross the finish line!

I became my first "client" using a holistic lifestyle to reach health goals. Since then, I have helped over 300 people transform their health through functional medicine. For a while I was still doing this as a "side gig" as I was still working full-time in the hospital and was not yet looking for an exit strategy. Well, that didn't last too long. Just in time, when I was hitting another rock bottom, and now experiencing burnout for the second time in 4 short years, I found myself in the same exact place confused and overwhelmed. I was, again, asking myself, "Is this it?" Is this what I am meant to be doing for the rest of my life until I retire? I felt so out of balance and unsettled because deep down, I knew I was meant for so much more. I just didn't know what it was going to look like until one day I heard a podcast that changed my life.

My commute used to take over 2 hours a day, most of which was sitting in traffic, and I listened to podcasts to kill time rather than listening to the radio. One evening, as I was driving home and trying to keep my eyes open after a very stressful evening shift at the hospital, I turned on a podcast where a Nurse Practitioner was sharing her story about how she went from traditional medicine into functional medicine and now has her own online practice. This happened to be the same day I was introduced to Karissa Kouchis (KK), a master coach who worked with Tony Robbins. Listening to these women and their stories, I felt like they were speaking straight to my soul. I heard terms like "time freedom," "working from home," and "making an impact in the world." I was eager to learn more, so I started asking questions like, how does this online practice work? What training and certifications are needed? Will the California Board of Pharmacy allow me to have my own practice? I mean, a million questions passed through my mind. These were all questions that I have never thought of asking myself, so it felt strange to even think about starting my own business. This was a huge investment, and I started to ask myself, "What happens if I fail?"

It was January 2020, and something inside me switched on and suddenly my soul was on fire. I just knew this was going to be my year. Again, in order to make big, bold decisions, I needed to be surrounded by mentors. I needed a tribe that would elevate me so I could unleash my full potential! I invested in my very first personal development program with KK and became a founding member of the Unleash Her Power Within (UHPW) tribe. At the same time, I also decided to hire my very first business coach and joined a mastermind, learning all about entrepreneurship as a virtual Functional Medicine Practitioner. During that mastermind, I met some women who have become my new best friends. They are Nurse Practitioners and Physician Associates, who are now some of the co-authors in this book.

I manifested leaving my job for my 40th birthday and created my own online legacy. 2020 was that year. Like many clinicians who pivot, I was so scared. What if I fail? What if this is not going to work out? I started doubting myself as to if I knew enough to have my own practice. I was second guessing myself and wondering if I made the right decision in hiring someone I just met. Then I remembered why I hired my business coach in the first place, and I kept going. I did this because my *why* was so strong. I no longer wanted to choose between family and career, as I knew it was possible to have both.

In March 2020, the global pandemic quickly proved that I was making the right investments and decisions for my life. The world was changing so quickly. Overnight, telemedicine and online virtual practice became the new normal. I quickly realized how much I had to learn and how fast I needed to implement everything I had been learning. As a clinical pharmacist, I was trained in the acute care hospital setting for 13 years, and now I had to shift my focus to preventative medicine using functional medicine. There was a tight deadline to get things in order because I was set to launch my practice in May. I also made a decision to go back to school and take online classes that were functional medicine specific. There was a lot on my plate, but I stayed laser focused on my vision and nothing could distract me. I was like one of those racing horses with their side blinders on, running in one lane, fast and with intention. I learned how to own my worth and charge for my services and my consultations. All of this to become a business owner, functional medicine practitioner, and coach.

There was an opportunity in my profession as a pharmacist that many haven't thought about. I saw an opportunity for growth and an exit strategy if the pandemic was going to last longer than anticipated. Creating my own virtual Functional Medicine Practice during the pandemic became my goal so I could fully walk away from the corporate world. I finally figured out the solution to my health, lifestyle, and career problems. I could now work from home as my own boss, without sacrificing my income at all, and I could do all this by launching my own virtual Functional Medicine Practice. Once again, I felt so accomplished. I created something, without knowing exactly how it would happen, and let the desire to rewrite my story guide my way. I knew I would have many challenges along the way, and I was OK with that. It was a bold decision, and it was something that the real-life Wonder Woman would do, so I did it.

On May 11th, 2020, I launched my Functional Medicine Practice. This was exactly 5 years after starting my own health transformation journey. I continued working limited hours on the weekends at the hospital, in addition to my job. I realized that our childcare situation wasn't perfect, but we made it work as long as we could. Until, one day in late May, I was informed that my work schedule could not be accommodated any longer, and that I needed to go back to work full-time starting in June. Telling our kids that we had to hire a nanny, a complete stranger from an agency, so I could go back to work, was one of the hardest days of the pandemic. Both kids cried and asked questions like, "Why are you leaving us?" "What if this person hurts us?" "What if we get sick?" and "Why is work more important than us?" I cried as I tried to comfort them, saying "Everything will be OK" and "We will get through this together." It was so hard that I couldn't sleep for many days. I had to choose to go back to work, as working from home was not an option, and I wasn't ready to leave my job. In my mind, I was still waiting for the "perfect time" to leave, meaning I didn't have the mindset that was necessary in order to make changes right at that moment, and not wait any longer. It was so hard, knowing I had no other options but to leave the kids and go back to work full-time.

> *"When we least expect it, life sets us a challenge to test our courage and willingness to change; at such a moment, there is no point in pretending that nothing has happened or in saying that we are not yet ready. The challenge will not wait. Life does not look back. A week is more than enough time for us to decide whether or not to accept our destiny."*
>
> – Paulo Coelho

Even though I had technically launched my functional medicine practice, at that time, it was only a "side gig." I quickly realized that having one foot in my own practice, and one foot in my corporate career was not serving anybody well, especially myself and my family. I was only doing a half-ass job and was not able to generate the amount of income (or impact) needed to turn my side-gig into a full-time job, not while still working full-time as a pharmacist, at least. A month or so into trying to balance both, I couldn't tolerate the pain any longer. I had to make a decision and move forward. More decisions to make at just the right time when I was hitting yet another rock bottom. In July 2020, I decided to attend a virtual event by Tony Robbins called Unleash the Power Within (UPW). My kids saw me go through a transformational breakthrough. They heard me speak my goals out loud and knew that I was working to find a way to work from home so I wouldn't have to choose between family and career. This event changed my life. It was there that I gained clarity of what I wanted to do, in large part because I was surrounded by others who were hungry for growth as much as I was. I broke through my fears of failure, by physically breaking a board in half! On one side of the board, I wrote "Fear of Failure" and the other side I wrote, "I am unstoppable, I am Wonder Woman." During this virtual event, I met someone very special, an incredible female CEO that soon became my role model. I was so inspired by an interview Tony Robbins did with Sara Blakely, inventor of Spanx, that I got full-body chills listening to her story. Her passion and drive moved me to make a difference in this world and support other female entrepreneurs along the way. I found my calling and got the guts to pursue my passion and purpose and to help other women rewrite their stories and become the best version of themselves too! It was the perfect timing in my life to reclaim my purpose and focus on making a difference in this world. I finally realized that in order to truly rewrite my story, I had to put two feet into my functional medicine practice, and work through the uncomfortable feelings associated with the risk. I knew it would be worth it in the end and I knew the decision I was about to make would even further change my life, and that I would be helping others change their lives along the way.

Come August 2020, and my kids were starting online school, just like the majority of kids in 2020. Knowing I had no reliable childcare, I made the terrifying decision to take a huge pay cut and walk away from my full-time job. This was the most stable job I had ever had, as I had been working there for over a decade, post residency training. Letting go of my job allowed me to focus 100% on my family and in my new practice. I walked away from my 6-figure career and reputation as a leading pharmacist, to step into the space of entrepreneurship.

This pandemic made me realize just how quickly our lives can change and how much we can do to change our lives if we have a burning desire to pursue our purpose. Walking away from security and moving forward without the answers totally goes against my life-long pharmacist training of doing the research before taking action. It was scary, but also so exciting. And it all just felt so right.

> *"The only thing keeping you from getting what you want is the story you keep telling yourself about why you can't have it. Break free!"*
> – Tony Robbins

After leaving my job at the end of August 2020, I spent the entire month of September slowing down and catching up with life. I will never forget the feeling of waking up the following morning and feeling free! I felt like 1,000 pounds of weight was lifted off my shoulders. I wasn't rushing anywhere; I wasn't hitting the snooze on the alarm over and over. There was nowhere to go other than being present with my family. That morning, I became a full-time mom for the very first time in all of our lives. It happened to be a very special day too because I got to witness my son receive his black belt in Taekwondo. I sat back, thinking about how I had been a part-time mom for over a decade, and I was always missing out on first events and milestones. Instead, I was either stuck in traffic and couldn't make it home on time, or I was working the weekend and missing out on family time together, making memories. The moment I realized I no longer have to ask anyone how I should spend my day was such a monumental accomplishment. Witnessing my son earn his black belt was the cherry on top of it all. We both accomplished something that was scary and took a lot of grit to accomplish. It was hard work, but we did it!

The reason I am sharing all these details is that they each played a key part in my story. We are often told things like, "everything will work out" and "everything happens for a reason." I believe this is true, even though we may not see or understand it at the moment. Remember, my health transformation started in 2015 after hearing my doctor tell me I would have a heart attack within 5 years if I didn't start taking a pill and losing weight. Honestly, if my doctor didn't use those words to "scare" me, I wouldn't have taken my health as seriously as I did. I wouldn't have immediately looked for a better way to take care of my health. I wouldn't have found holistic health. I wouldn't have found my tribe and community who continues to inspire me every single day. Everything does happen for a reason, and at just the right time in our lives. Those painful moments in life lead to lessons that teach you something that you will understand later.

If you are experiencing rejection from something you have worked so hard for, consider it to be a redirection towards your next big thing. I have been rejected several times, two of which I will never forget. First, I was rejected from multiple pharmacy schools in California, only to be put on a waitlist with no hope of getting in. Then, I moved all the way to Florida, only to find out that same day that one of the schools in California actually decided to accept me. Frustration and confusion could have set in, but instead, I knew there was a reason I went to school in Florida. If I hadn't made the scary decision to move to Florida, I would never have met a few of the other authors of this book. There is a reason I was rejected from a position I applied for within my pharmacy department. If I had started with that position, it would have kept me in the same place for many years instead of stepping into something that's my real purpose. It's no secret that life will suck sometimes. At times, it may seem unfair, but always look for lessons learned and trust the path you are being redirected to. Stay the course, your course, and all really will work out in the end.

When I made the conscious decision to slow down and take the entire month of September off, I began manifesting and visualizing how I would be spending my days, where I would focus my energy, and how I could serve those who need me the most. When I launched my online practice, I focused on helping women with weight loss, detoxifying their bodies, gaining energy, and reducing stress. Those were my main pillars of health that I knew for a fact would change their lives. In addition to these pillars, I offered functional medicine specific lab testing to take the guesswork out and focus on the root cause. I knew the universe needed my services, I knew there are women who are struggling and desperately looking for solutions that I could offer. Part of me kept holding me back on going all in and scaling my clinical services because I found myself having dozens of conversations with other burnout pharmacists who were in the exact same shoes as I was. They were also stuck between two worlds, choosing between their career that no longer fulfilled them, and their family that needed them the most. Hearing my colleagues go through the same pain and struggle, I knew I had to provide them with a solution and help them out in a way that nobody else has yet to offer. At this time, I had many tearful conversations with colleagues and other pharmacists who wanted to know how they could also reclaim their lives. Many of these people were moms who were in very similar shoes as I was. They were stressed, overwhelmed, and overworked, while also not making the impact on their patients that they desperately longed for. These conversations made me realize that I needed to invest into my own growth, so I could show up for these women and be able to lead as their mentor as their business coach.

Days later, as I allowed the universe to tell me what my next "big step" was going to look like, I met my mentor, Rebecca Cafiero. I joined her mastermind along with 20 other female entrepreneurs. Being in that group, and finding my tribe, changed my life in a way that ultimately is working to change other women's lives as well. I worked really hard to find the best platform for my network of clinicians to learn about functional medicine without feeling overwhelmed. It was my goal to help them create their own functional medicine legacy. Again, I made a decision to only work with a handful of clinical clients and spend my time and energy preparing to launch the *Functional Medicine Business Academy*™ (FMBA).

On November 11th, 2020, FMBA came to fruition. There was something special about the date 11-11, and I knew how special this academy and our tribe was going to be. I knew it had to be unique and different. It took me about 6 months of constant research, collaboration, and strategy to add more and more value to FMBA until it was finally ready to be presented as the world's first Functional Medicine Certification Program. The Functional Medicine Business Academy™ is a business incubator for clinicians to launch and scale their functional medicine practice while simultaneously working to become a Certified Functional Medicine Specialist™. I knew how important certification is in the medical world and how important it was to merge clinical mentorship with business mentorship.

Unlike other functional medicine certification programs that only focus on clinical skills, the Functional Medicine Business Academy™ provides both clinical and entrepreneurial skills in addition to the certification. This is a business accelerator for "business athletes" as my mentor and my next business coach, Kelly Roach, likes to say. Imagine if we all went to pharmacy school without any rotations. And once we graduate and pass the boards, we are expected to work, be a leading pharmacist, manage technicians, clerks, and the rest of the support staff. There is a reason we have clinical rotations while in pharmacy school. Rotations give you exposure and teach you how to "practice as a pharmacist" once you are licensed. That's the exact model that occurs now in all other functional medicine programs. You are expected to learn all the clinical stuff and then are set free to somehow figure out how to start your practice. This leaves people confused and overwhelmed, without the skills to get paid for your services or the resources and network to grow and scale your practice. Trust me, I know it can feel overwhelming. That's exactly how I felt. And it's precisely why I had to create this business incubator with the clinical skills and business skills we all need to be successful practitioners. Let me tell you, there is something magical about being surrounded by a like-minded badass tribe!

As a mentor and leader in functional medicine, I always look for opportunities to make this world a better place. Every year, I set huge goals that naturally feel uncomfortable. I push past that feeling, however, because I set goals that are aligned with my vision and purpose. As I said before, last year on 11-11, I launched the *Functional Medicine Business Academy*™ and this year on that exact date, I am launching STORRIE™ Wellness. STORRIE™ Wellness is a virtual wellness center in which all the clinicians I work with through the FMBA have the chance to practice functional medicine together, through a shared vision of changing lives and healing people to truly heal from within. As a wellness center, I am also working on launching a professional-grade organic supplement and CBD line.

I'll leave you with a few of my final thoughts. First, it's not all about achieving a goal, it's about who you become in the process of pursuing your goals. You want to be proud of the person you have worked hard to become. Next, always remember that you are resilient. You have already conquered so much throughout your life, and you are more than capable to withstand the challenges that come along with making healthy changes. Last but not least, be patient with your transformation and have the courage to say "YES!" to the right opportunities. With dedication, community, and a strong work ethic, you will know when it's time for *you* to Unleash the STORRIE™ Within, and maybe that time is *now*!

> *"The struggle you're in today is developing the strength you need for tomorrow."*
> – ROBERT TEW

ABOUT DR. CHRISTINE MANUKYAN

Dr. Christine Manukyan is a Functional Medicine Practitioner, Business Coach, Bestselling Author, Speaker, Top-Rated STORRIE™ Podcast host and mother of two. Prior to becoming an entrepreneur, she spent 13 years in Corporate America as a Clinical Pharmacist with various leadership roles. After experiencing her own health transformation with Functional Medicine, losing 100+ lbs. and becoming a natural bodybuilding athlete and marathon runner, she found her true calling empowering others to reach their health goals without pharmaceuticals. Dr. Christine has helped more than 300 clients transform their health and has certified/mentored 30+ clinicians as Certified Functional Medicine Specialists™. She is a lifelong learner and is currently enrolled in Functional Medicine University (FMU) and The School of Applied Functional Medicine (SAFM).

Dr. Christine is the Founder and CEO of the *Functional Medicine Business Academy™* and *STORRIE™ Wellness*. She is a frequent speaker on holistic lifestyle choices, creating a virtual business, founder and entrepreneur mindset and creating multiple income streams. She's spoken in front of audiences numbering 15,000+ and has been recognized globally for her entrepreneurial achievement and dedication. Her past publications and magazine features include Yahoo, Disruptors, The NYC Journal, Functional Medicine Pharmacists Magazine, SHEFIND, and she is a BRAINZ Magazine Executive Contributor, including BRAINZ 500 Global recognition.

Dr. Christine is passionate about coaching burned-out medical professionals struggling to balance family, career, and their health to take control of their life and career and create a profitable virtual practice with her signature The INTEGRATE Method™.

She believes everyone deserves a second chance to rewrite their STORRIE™ and become the best version of themselves.

www.drchristinemanukyan.com | drchristine@storrie.co | IG: @dr.christine.manukyan

Chapter 2

THE PATH TOWARDS HEALING AND EMPOWERMENT

By Allie Burch MSN, FNP-C, MCN, IFMCP

> *"When we have the courage to walk into our story and own it, we get to write the ending."*
> – Brene Brown

As we continue to be in the middle of a global pandemic, with COVID-19, many people have shifted their health priorities. Since the Covid-19 virus puts those with chronic illnesses (even those with a vitamin D deficiency), more at risk of severe illness, this pandemic has shined a brighter light on the poor health status of our country. This is not new information, but the lay person and conventional providers now seem to be paying more attention. As for me, as a holistic practitioner, the poor health status of our country has been a huge driving force for the work I choose to do. It is one of the primary reasons I have chosen the career path I have. Another reason I chose the path I did, was due to my own personal experiences. From a young age, I saw the disconnect that the medical community had when it came to treating chronic illnesses and symptoms of dysfunction. I recognized that there is no true model for preventative care and what does exist is truly lacking in so many areas.

When I was 17, I became a mother. From that point on, I became a health warrior, seeking information to create a healthy environment and lifestyle for myself and my family. What I found was that my trusted medical providers did not have the information or answers I was seeking, and that was a huge motivator for me to become a leader in the holistic medicine realm, so I could help myself and others.

I feel that my own personal health awareness and journey started when I became pregnant as a teenager. It was hard to be a teenage mother on many levels, but I ultimately became responsible for this other life, and I wanted to do my best to be a good mother. I started to think about how I was raised. My mother was conscious of reducing sugar in our diets, she grew a garden when we were young, and made most of our meals from scratch. It definitely created a foundation in my relationship with food, especially, as I myself became a parent. I also became aware of all the chemicals in our environment that we come in contact with, and that were considered to be an acceptable part of daily living. This fascinated me, as well as concerned me, that most Americans were exposed to these toxic substances constantly. I will never forget taking my daughter to daycare and watching the employee spray down the table with a blue chemical cleaner, then placing their snack on that table. I asked very nicely to please not use the cleaner, thinking to myself, "What's wrong with soap and water?" And then I suggested they use a plate. I was made to feel like I was a difficult parent. As my awareness grew and I became more educated in living a more natural life, I was often made to feel wrong for my standards and was very often given the eye roll. I don't think I was ever preachy or rude, I was just concerned, and tried to create a standard of reducing toxins from our environment in both food, cleaning, and body products. That's not the norm, though, right? At least it wasn't in 1994. Over the last 27 years, I have watched the world shift towards understanding these principles more, and I believe we are now seeing a wellness revolution occur. We still have a long way to go, of course, and all you have to do is walk into a grocery store and look around, as 80-90% of what is in the grocery store is either not real food or has chemical ingredients that have been shown to be harmful to the human body. It's sad and unfortunate, but it's the truth, and there is now research to show these chemicals are linked to many diseases and illnesses. Even today, I find that most people are not educated, or do not want to fully believe that what they purchase in a store is not safe. This is one of the foundations to the work I do now with people, which helps them reduce their toxic load in multiple areas of their day-to-day lives.

Another defining point in my life was when my children were young, I was a single parent living on WIC and food stamps. I was required to be in a program where I would check in for health visits, and my children would get assessed and weighed. It was also meant to be educational and supportive for parents. I met a nurse practitioner who praised me for my efforts in clean living and encouraged me. It was her interaction, kind words, compassion, and recognition that inspired me to be interested in becoming a nurse practitioner. It wasn't until 10 years later, I would go to school for nursing, but I never forgot her praise and remember feeling validated and encouraged by her words. I felt like I was on the right track and maybe I was one of the few who cared about healthy living, but I wasn't the only one and I knew it mattered. That is the power of education. So simple, but it made such an impression on me, that being validated for my healthy lifestyle choices made me realize I wanted to help others do the same.

Another defining point for me in my life was during my own personal health journey. I struggled with my own health when I was pregnant with my third child. I thought I was very healthy. I was only 24 years old. I was a pescatarian, mostly eating a vegetarian diet, thinking that I had a healthy diet, but was still gaining a lot of pregnancy weight. I had to eat every two to three hours, and didn't feel well when I skipped a meal, which wasn't anything new, but seemed to be more of an issue during this pregnancy. I was diagnosed with pre-gestational diabetes. It didn't make any sense to me, as I was young and healthy, and thought I had a very healthy diet. After my son was born, I had a hard time losing my pregnancy weight. I continued to have to snack every few hours or else I would feel my blood sugar dropping. It was even a joke in my family because I brought snacks everywhere. I visited with my general practitioner, who told me maybe it was because I was breastfeeding, and I needed more calories. He also acknowledged that I was at higher risk of someday developing type two diabetes as reflected by my pregnancy blood work. Her recommendations were to continue eating every two to three hours, eat a healthy amount of carbs to stabilize my blood sugar, and come back in a year for blood work. I continued to feel unwell, tired, and fatigued, and I never could skip a meal. I always had a normal hemoglobin (A1C), but many years later, and through my own health research, I learned this was the wrong way to treat insulin resistance. It wasn't until later that I realized that insulin resistance was what I was experiencing. Through my own discovery about newer research and methods in treating insulin resistance, I was able to treat myself and reverse my insulin resistance through fasting and a low-carb diet. I continue to follow this eating plan today and have had great success with it. Unfortunately, my medical provider was unable to support me and had no knowledge of how to help, other than telling me to continue to eat every 2-3 hours. I continue to see this type of interaction today, leaving many patients feeling stuck and not getting the results that they are seeking. Unfortunately, most conventional medical providers are not giving accurate advice and do not have the knowledge in how to help people with one of the most prominent chronic illnesses we, as a society, suffer from: obesity, insulin resistance, and type two diabetes. These have become the issues I am driven to help people get the information about so they, too, can change their life's trajectory towards a path of health and away from illness.

Early in my career, prior to becoming a nurse practitioner, I became a licensed massage therapist and practiced as a doula. I had an intense drive to learn more about the human body and medicine. I wanted to help change the medical community from the inside out. To do this, I knew I needed more training, and I knew I wanted to be a holistic nurse practitioner but didn't have a clear vision how this would manifest until many years later. I started off at community college, with three small children at home, and worked my way through nursing school, eventually graduating with my associate degree. Then, I continued on to pursue my Bachelors, while working as an ICU Registered Nurse, before going on to completing my master's degree to become a family nurse practitioner (NP). After graduating and passing my board certification, I worked as a hospitalist NP for a total of 7 years. A few years after starting clinical practice as a Hospitalist, I went back for a second master's in clinical nutrition and started studying functional medicine through the Institute of Functional Medicine (IFM). This helped me to slowly move towards my original professional interests, which was to become a holistic practitioner. Even with my passion and drive to practice more natural medicine, it was important to me to understand the conventional clinical medical model. I wanted to learn about disease processes and treatments. I believe we frequently need to blend both traditional and holistic medicine. I also knew if I was going to change the system, I really needed to understand clinical medicine and gain the respect of other conventional practitioners. In total, I stayed in the hospital setting for 12 years. What I saw was that modern medicine is amazing and lifesaving, most of the time! When it comes to emergent and acute illnesses, we are extremely lucky to have access to well-trained medical providers, advanced techniques, and modern medicine. Where it fails is managing and reversing chronic illnesses. I can't even count the number of patients I had who were taking 20 to 30 medications a day at home. People are chronically sick, and it has become a vicious cycle. Obviously, so many factors go into this. But what I saw in the hospital setting was we could do better, as a system, to teach people better lifestyle skills. We could do better in the outpatient primary care model to help people improve their lives and reverse their illnesses.

Let's talk about the food we serve in the hospital setting. Aren't we supposed to be a model for health? Post heart attack patients are still eating cake, muffins, greasy burgers, and they don't know any better. I'll never forget a 50-year-old, Type-2 diabetic patient, that I admitted for an infected diabetic ulcer on his foot, which later required amputation. He had just lost 50 lbs. in 6 months, just by changing his diet to a whole foods diet. One morning, I was doing rounds, and I happened to be there when his breakfast tray came. I watched his face as he looked at what he was being served, and I'll never forget his look of horror. A bagel and cream cheese, blueberry muffin, orange juice, eggs, sausage, and potatoes. This was the "consistent carb diet" we serve to diabetic patients in the hospital. As I apologized and agreed with him that we are still stuck in 1970, we worked on getting him some lower carb, healthier foods, such as replacing his potatoes with low-carb vegetables. I've raised concerns to the dietitians, as well as administration, but my thoughts and concerns fell on deaf ears. These were the national recommendations after all. These experiences I've had while working in the hospital have shaped who I am today and continue to drive me to interrupt healthcare by openly talking about these issues with my colleagues and creating a clinical practice where people can be educated about healthy lifestyle, and giving others the steps so they can put these things into practice

I am very passionate about helping people reverse or at least improve their chronic illnesses or vague symptoms that leave them feeling unwell. After all, this is our *one life,* and we deserve to feel well and live a full life! I hear too often from people that they are "just getting older" or "my mom has the same thing, it's in my genes." We now know that most chronic illnesses are secondary to poor lifestyle routines, such as eating too much ultra-processed foods, sugar, and unhealthy fats, as well as a sedentary lifestyle, poor sleep habits, stress, smoking, alcohol, etc. It is no doubt a complex problem that runs deep and has multiple factors that play a role, but the reality is, most people who have chronic illnesses would benefit from lifestyle changes. This has been shown in the new clinical research that *The Cleveland Clinic* has been conducting. Their functional medicine clinic, which was started in 2014, is showing that 80% of people who go through a 6-week lifestyle course do not need to see a medical provider. I find this to be true in my own clinical practice, and that 80% of people I work with will get better when they start incorporating healthy lifestyle routines into their life. The other 20% usually require a deep dive into more in-depth, out-of-box testing, such as, assessing full hormone and thyroid panel, advanced metabolic, gut, and nutrient testing. These things we generally do not assess in our current standard clinical model. This approach and these tools have been taught to me in my advanced training and have drastically changed my patients' outcome.

Did you know that the Centers for Disease and Control (CDC) and the World Health Organization (WHO), state that most chronic illnesses can be prevented, and many of them are reversible? This is not new information. Where is the model to teach people and support them in our current clinical medical offices, though? Why are our current medical practices so far behind the newer research? These are questions I ask myself frequently.

I like talking about data because the proof is there and it is eye-opening, when put in perspective. Chronic illnesses are a pandemic. In the U.S. alone, chronic illnesses are out of control. 42% of adults are obese, and obesity affects 1 in 6 children. Let's stop and say that again. Almost half of U.S. adults are obese! Our children are following right behind. This is not about vanity. Obesity is linked to dozens of chronic illnesses. Obesity was rare in the 1950s, which isn't that long ago. What about other diseases? One in two Americans has a chronic illness, and one in four has multiple. Almost 70 percent of Americans take at least one prescription, and more than half take at least two. Seventy-four percent of doctors' visits end in a prescription being written and approximately 2.9 billion drugs are being prescribed a year, according to the CDC. The U.S. spends more on healthcare than any other wealthy country, yet our outcomes are worse. Most functional medicine providers understand the broken system, and these statistics are partially what drives their pursuit to deliver a better model.

So, what is functional medicine? The Functional Medicine Model, as defined by the IFM, states, "Functional medicine determines how and why illness occurs and restores health by addressing the root causes of disease for each individual. The functional medicine model is an individualized, patient-centered, science-based approach that empowers patients and practitioners to work together to address underlying causes of disease and promote optimal wellness." In my opinion, this is the change in medicine we need in order to budge the needle in the right direction instead of in the direction we have been going. This model empowers the patient to learn, become educated, and take control.

As I enter my 5th year of my functional medicine practitioner journey, I can honestly say that I am as passionate now, if not more, than I was when I first discovered it. That says a lot because when I first discovered functional medicine, it was as if the universe aligned. I was hooked the first time I heard Jeff Bland, PhD (a.k.a. the father of functional medicine) speak. He so brilliantly and eloquently connected the dots of what is wrong with our current health care approach, in regard to chronic illnesses, and developed a model that looks at the body as a whole. Functional Medicine integrates a system that aims to identify the root cause of illness or dysfunction. It presents a different paradigm of how to understand disease and health, and this immediately resonated with me. It was the missing link in the broken chain of creating actual change.

Disease, or one's symptoms, is always pointing to a disordered function in the body. It is a smoke signal telling us something is wrong. Therefore, the goal of treatment should be based on restoring function. One of the key foundations of functional medicine is lifestyle including, nutrition, sleep, movement, stress, reducing environmental exposures, as well as psycho-spiritual aspects of our lives. It is also taking an in-depth look at their past medical history, from birth to present, and looking at the whole picture. Something that, normally, is not included in our current model. These simple, yet powerful tools, have been some of the best game changers in my clinical practice, with patients consistently having successful outcomes.

There are two patients I want to tell you about that changed everything for me. I'll never forget one of the first patients I worked with. Her story will forever be a catalyst for me in being excited about this model, for being enraged with our current broken medical model, and for sparking the fire within me to disrupt healthcare and continue to practice and share this work. She was a 32-year-old successful Psychologist, with her own private practice. In her late 20s, she was diagnosed with rheumatoid arthritis. She was monitored by a rheumatologist and primary care provider closely and was on immunosuppressive medications. She came to me desperate, stating she had so much pain that she was considering going on disability. She was told that since her grandmother had rheumatoid arthritis, it had to be genetic, and therefore there was not much to do about it but treat with immunosuppressive and anti-inflammatory therapy. She had already tried other alternative healing modalities such as acupuncture, massage therapy and had previously worked with a registered dietician without much success. First, we started with an elimination diet with a focus on an autoimmune protocol, removing foods that are known to interact with the immune system. The elimination diet is the gold standard for food sensitivity evaluation. There should always be a focus on nutrient dense, whole food eating, and not just restricting. We did a broad panel of blood work which did show micronutrient deficiencies, such as, magnesium, zinc, vitamin D, and omega 3's. She had signs of elevated inflammatory markers. In my first visit, I also educate and encourage patients to reduce their toxic loads by cleaning up their environment. This includes food quality, household, and beauty products, while also working on daily detox support. We discussed the importance of sleep, stress reduction, mindset, as well as the importance of our psycho-social-spiritual health and community. At our 6-week follow-up, she walked in, beaming like she was a completely different person, stating her pain was 100% gone. I will never forget the moment she told me this, in my office, with tears in her eyes. She had *hope*. She felt *empowered*. She was *pain free*. It was at that moment that I realized it was my responsibility to share what I have learned with whoever will listen. Of course, it is not always that easy, but over and over again, I see people improving and resolving their chronic illnesses/symptoms of dysfunction with simple lifestyle changes and support. I watch their life trajectory shift from a path of illness, towards a path of *healing* and *empowerment*.

The second patient I want to tell you about is a 56-year-old female who came to see me with concerns about her diagnosis of obesity, type-two diabetes, chronic joint pain, and fatigue. She was on disability at the time and wanted to get her health back so she could work and be active with her grandchildren. She was very poor and had little resources. She took in everything we discussed in our first visit and by the second visit, 4-5 weeks later, she had completed an elimination diet, lost 10 lbs., and had less pain and fatigue. She could not believe it! She could not afford to buy a lot of groceries, so she grew a garden with vegetables, including a lot of green leafy vegetables, in her apartment complex. Six months later she lost 30 lbs., had no joint pain, did not need the assistance of her cane, and was able to come off her metformin (her diabetes medication). She also started working three days a week in a job she loved.

I have now treated hundreds of patients using this model and have seen, firsthand, how it can be life changing for someone. The excitement and joy I get when I see someone has shifted their path of illness towards health, is incredible. Seeing that they have reversed their chronic disease or symptoms and have shifted their long-term health trajectory to one of wellness and a longer health span, is absolutely astounding. I always tell my patients that I am just merely the guide and their cheerleader. They are the ones who have decided that it is important and have taken the time to educate themselves and have done the work. This is true empowerment.

The model of functional medicine, in my opinion, is one of the answers to truly changing the broken model of health care as we know it. We currently live in a "sick care model" where we treat "an ill with a pill," as Dr. Mark Hyman says. The current model is broken. Period. The question is now, what are we, as healthcare providers, going to do about it?

We can't keep doing the same thing over and over and expecting different outcomes. This is a mindset that has helped me shift many things in my life. One of the things I am very proud of, and a time when I took my own advice, is when I quit my corporate medicine job in the summer of 2021. I do try to walk the talk, but this was a hard, big decision in my life. I was working at the hospital while running my private practice but was always being pulled in different directions. I recognized that things were not aligning, and I was putting my own health at risk. I guess I am not a superhuman after all! But it was more than that. The stress of working in the hospital, in a fear-based job and environment, was overwhelming. It was affecting my own health in negative ways, and I was plunging myself into that environment 10 days a month, and it would typically take me four days to recover afterwards. I also was watching most of, if not all, my medical colleagues suffer from burnout. Since leaving, my private practice has flourished. I feel that I am finally the curator to my future in both my health and business. I am practicing not only what I am passionate about and believe in, but also have made the space to be creative. I have continued to surround myself with a like-minded community and have developed deep friendships and found brilliant mentors. I am here to show that you can have a messy, imperfect life, but don't stop fighting for your passion and dreams, listen to your gut feeling, and fight for what you know to be true. I have found my own empowerment and healing along the way and am now living in alignment with what I believe in, and I know you can too.

ABOUT ALLIE BURCH

Allie Burch is a Board-Certified Family Nurse Practitioner, holding two Master's Degrees in Nursing and Clinical Nutrition. She has extensive experience as a hospitalist as well, and early in her career as a Licensed Massage Therapist and Doula, prior to pursuing an education in nursing. Allie's specialty is in Functional Medicine, where she has trained through the Institute of Functional Medicine, in which the model focuses on individualized, patient-centered, science-based approaches that addresses the underlying causes of disease and promotes optimal wellness. In 2021, Allie left her corporate hospitalist job and committed to her virtual practice full-time. She is now running a successful functional medicine membership model where she continues to help people reach optimal wellness, increase longevity, and overall health span. Check out Allie's website for information, and make sure to join her mailing list for free resources and virtual support.

www.allieburch.com | allie@allieburch.com | IG: @allie.burch

Chapter 3

TURNING DOWN THE WHITE NOISE

By Angela S. Garcia, PharmD, MPH, CPh

"It is worth remembering that the time of greatest gain in terms of wisdom and inner strength is often that of greatest difficulty."

– Dalai Lama

My functional medicine journey begins with finally trusting myself enough to walk away from dysfunctional medicine and the prison it created for me in managing my disease. *My* disease. It honestly sounds weird to me to own that. But it's the truth, it's mine. It is mine to own, to control, and to train my body to manage. Not just to deal with it, but to live and thrive with it. Because of my faith, I have embodied a mantra based on 2 Corinthians 2:5 which reads, "We take captive every thought and make it obedient to Christ." My approach is that I will take captive my disease and bring it under my control. As for me and my story, battle, and victory, spiritual health is the core foundation of my approach to medicine which allows me to function and live. I have always had a deep sense of faith and spirituality, even as a child. There is no question that I have experienced the power of God's ultimate healing multiple times in my life. He has perfectly designed all our bodies, when aligned and treated with no stone unturned, He will give us the power to overcome any disease.

For most people, there is not a conscious thought to breathing. It's not even something you consider. It is happening without any thought. But for me, it was something I had to think about. I had a constant awareness of the slightest change in my breathing. It was like white noise to me. If you don't know what white noise is, in the context of breathing, let me try to explain: White noise machines typically have a slight hum or buzz that helps to distract from other sounds or to create a rhythm that is almost hypnotic. This sound allows you to fade off into sleep, to buffer conversations from others, to create a soft subtle unrecognizable sound to shift the mind's ability to focus and be calm. Being constantly aware of my breathing was just like white noise. It was constant. I heard it. I felt it. I was always thinking about it. In the background of every single activity, whether engaged in physical exertion or relaxation, there was my breath. I felt trapped, restricted, and frustrated. Everyone else could wave off a smell or was seemingly unaffected by scents, odors, perfumes, deodorizers, smoke, and aeroallergens, basically anything you could breathe in. But for me, I noticed the smell before anyone else. I closed my eyes and waited to see if the tapping (wheezing) started in my chest and waited to see if bronchospasms (coughing or chest tightness) would begin. We were breathing the same air, but for some reason, my lungs just didn't work the same as everyone else's.

When I was in high school, it was very obvious my breathing was different from the way everyone one else was breathing. We all breathed hard after sprints, using ancillary muscles and movements to get more air into our lungs, and then deeply breathing out in order to make more room for air. After all of us took a few recovery breaths (deep breaths that slowed our respiratory and heart rates down) everyone else seemed to be ready for their next event. This was a bold realization that my lungs were not recovering. I wasn't taking functional breaths. I wasn't able to talk. I was posturing and struggling to the point where I couldn't even walk up the stairs to sit with my team in the bleachers after I raced. I had to stay on the grass inside the track and wait for my coach to bring my rescue inhaler or for the EMTs to bring me a nebulization treatment. It was through these experiences that I learned to recognize where I was in my crisis cycle based on how hard my body and lungs were working just to breathe.

    I want to share a quick history of myself. Many people claim to have the best parents, but I mean, who are we kidding? I was one of my parent's first children, so technically, they were still new to the whole parenting thing, so maybe they weren't the best? Just kidding! They are and always have been phenomenal people. I was fortunate enough to grow up in a home with both parents having graduate degrees (master's degrees) and working in education. My parents paved the way for me to have an unbelievably strong tie to my faith. They disciplined me, and now I strongly believe in discipline as loving correction. They taught me how to apologize and not just say the empty words of, "I'm sorry." They held me accountable, and were role models of integrity, faith, and a strong work ethic. My parents taught me about love in a marriage, in a family and in a relationship, whether friendship based or romantic. They taught me how to express myself and gave me a strong foundation. They let me make my own mistakes and they also allowed me to experience hurt, sadness, loneliness, knowing it would make me resilient. No matter how hard it was for them to watch me and my siblings struggle, they were well aware that it was part of healthy emotional development. I was taught how to express my anger appropriately (man those days were rough) and they taught me the dangers of harboring or expressing hate without safe boundaries. So, I can rightfully and without hesitation say my parents were not like everyone else's parents. I truly knew, with everything in me, they were different. They were the best parents ever. And they were mine.

While I was an undergrad, seeking my Bachelor of Psychology, I began to understand the concept of "quality of life." I hadn't really heard much of the term before then, but as soon as it was introduced, suddenly the white noise and the consciousness of my irregular breathing all made sense. I did not have the quality of life I wanted because I did not know how to control my asthma. I had no idea how to treat it, was tired of living with it, and I definitely didn't know how to control it. Because I didn't know, I was not living the life I could have been. When you have a chronic disease or syndrome, guess what happens.? You learn to be identified as your disease, and if you're not careful, you become defined by it too. I introduced myself as a disease. I would say, "I'm an asthmatic." Literally, I was saying, "I *am* asthma." I felt like I constantly had to give a reason for why my breathing was different or why they needed to be careful with me. I was not a person with asthma. I was asthma. And that is not wellness; that is sickness. And I had completely adopted a disease mindset.

In my childhood, my parents did not know what asthma was until I was in a crisis situation and heard for the first time, "Your daughter has asthma" from a doctor in the emergency room. That was basically the extent of what they knew about asthma and for a while, that's where it ended. My parents gave me the medicine the doctors recommended, until I looked like I was breathing better, and managed it just as they were taught. Oh wait, that's right, they were never taught about asthma, how to manage asthma, how to reduce the triggers of asthma, or how to assess when I was losing control and at risk for an exacerbation. They had no idea how my diagnosis was going to impact our family. When you are a child with a chronic disease, you begin to own things that are not yours to own. For example, I was the reason we had to rush to the hospital while everyone was running around scared and panicking. Sometimes scared adults sound like they are yelling at their children, but I didn't understand that they were just expressing their own fear until later in life. I was the reason my siblings had to stop having fun or not do certain things because it would trigger an asthmatic episode or reaction. I felt like a limitation to my family. I felt like it was all my fault. Not my chronic illness' fault, mine.

I hated that feeling, and I would do anything I could think of to not cause problems. I begged my brother not to tell on me when my wheezing was audible, because I knew what was going to happen after that. I caused problems. Those of us in the healthcare field understand that if you can audibly hear wheezing, the word "crisis" doesn't even come close to explaining the severity of the issues. It could be most closely explained as "life-threatening." No child, no family, and no parent should be in a situation where they are in the dark about a condition due to a lack of health literacy, resources, or education, and the full support of their healthcare team. Nobody should be held captive and powerless by a disease.

While sitting in an emergency department bed, mask on, medication dripping into my arm, I remember hearing something the doctor said to my parents that I will never forget, "One day you're not going to make it here in time. One day, she could die." My eyes began to well up with tears, and my parents were emotional. The doctor was honest and firm with his words, and I wasn't used to anyone being "firm with their words" toward my dad and him not responding. He was silenced, though. And I said, "I don't want to die," but no one heard me because the nebulized medication created too much white noise. I hate white noise.

Throughout the years, I had so many exacerbations, emergent interventions, rounds of medications, yet no one, not even once, ever sat with me or my parents to discuss the root causes of my asthma. Knowing the pathophysiology (physiological processes) of my asthma could determine what triggered my asthma, how to recognize and assess levels of control, and what options there were for treating my asthma. There was never any exploration across traditional, holistic, naturopathic, or other alternative medicine practices. There was no talk of spiritual healing, eating an anti-inflammatory diet, lung strengthening exercises, practicing mindfulness, breathing techniques, managing my environments, or any other approaches to care. If my parents were never taught and empowered, then how were they going to teach and empower me? My parents were formally educated, they were engaged, they were loving, and they were protective. However, they were not taught what they should know as parents with a child diagnosed with asthma. Unfortunately, that lack of asthma education almost killed me. More than once. Cats have nothing on me, I'm far beyond my nine lives and counting.

While playing sports in high school, my asthma became harder to manage and I knew sports in college was never going to happen. The problem was, I was very athletic, and I wanted to be strong physically, even though it was abundantly clear I could not compete with "normal athletes." By normal, I mean people that weren't classified as asthmatics. Sprints and dashes in track, softball, volleyball, and swimming were sports I could thrive in with the help of my trusty rescue inhaler, but there was always something in the way. It was that damn white noise. When I was in college, and no longer a contender for any sort of competitive sports, I found yoga, sort of. Everyone around me liked doing yoga with incense and candles, and I'm sorry, but when you can't breathe because of indoor air quality issues or other aeroallergens, then yoga in those environments was not an option. With yoga I found techniques that allowed me to breathe differently and feel differently, but I was not committed to it because everything about my breathing depended on something I couldn't control, the environment or the people around me. The environment was my enemy. Not knowing what my triggers were, or even understanding that concept, was keeping me imprisoned. Not knowing how I could control my asthma was the root of the power the environment had over me and my quality of life.

I'm going to go on record saying that children are so much more resilient than adults. You know why? Because they don't know about giving up. Their little bodies are just made to live and to thrive and to overcome. They are made to heal, grow, and develop. But when you grow up having a chronic disease, syndrome, or illness, it makes it so much harder to function without a disease mindset. I had made it to being an adult, but it's only by the grace of God I did not die from asthma during my childhood. I prayed when I was in that hospital bed with that mask on, "Please God, don't let me die!" Thankfully, that prayer was honored. I made it to adulthood, and things were becoming different. I learned some triggers to avoid, and I knew some of the triggers that made my asthma worse. I was beginning to learn to listen to my body and become aware of my environment. I would hear my body telling me when it was not breathing well and was going to force me into rest one way or another. Colds seemed to linger forever. Seasons changing were a signal for breathing problems to come. I got sick every year and it lasted for months. I had to avoid things I loved and people I wanted to hang out with, and I learned to just accept it. That was my life, and that was the life of many people with uncontrolled asthma.

A few years later, I developed a new white noise. It was my rescue inhaler. I knew I would die without it. That was the most dysfunctional of all relationships I had (and I had some doozies) but giving that rescue inhaler codependency up once and for all would take some convincing. I was headed to graduate school to earn my Doctor of Pharmacy, and knew it was about to create great change in my life. It was going to change my quality of life, and I thought it was going to finally educate me and train me all about my asthma. I was going to finally learn how to be in control of it. I started my first year of pharmacy school with experiential learning added to our core curriculum. I explored the American Lung Association, and it became an outlet in which I later became an Open Airways facilitator and local consortium member. We went to schools to teach children with and without asthma all about asthma. They were learning signs, symptoms, triggers, and how to explain to adults around them what was happening so they could communicate while struggling with their breathing and prevent emergencies.

    I cried after my training, because for the first time in my life, I fully understood what I had been missing in my care from my providers, and that there was a different life waiting for me. I could talk to the children in a language they understood. I used descriptions they would be able to identify with. I used terms like, "scratching on the inside of your throat and/or the front of your neck," "feeling tapping on the inside of your chest near your sternum," "sounding like a cat was inside your chest," or "feeling exhausted for no reason" or "feeling like you were standing in the pool trying to breathe as deep as you did standing outside the pool." This was my new tribe. These were my little people, and I was going to educate them over the next several weeks on each of the components of the asthma education program. I was going to empower them. I was going to do everything in my power to make sure no one was going to live with the same white noise that I did. Not if I could help it.

Over the next couple of years, I began learning about therapeutics, physiology, pathophysiology, and pharmacology. I was so astounded by the body and its desire to thrive, even as an adult. I developed the determination to become the best asthma clinician/educator, and I knew I was going to have a major role in asthma care and management as a career. This was my disease, after all, and this was my chance to turn this disease into the very reason I would thrive one day as a clinician. I knew I would practice respiratory care, somewhere, somehow. The only problem was, there was no specialty for pharmacists in asthma. I thought to myself, "What the hell? Cardiology, endocrinology, oncology, all the "ologies," but not respiratory?" Maybe if it were called "respirology" there would have been some kind of specialty offered, but there wasn't.

During my third year of pharmacy school, I had a water leak in the wall of my condo. Actually, a water fountain is a more accurate description. My upstairs neighbor was remodeling their bathroom and the plumber broke a pipe that was causing water to pour out through my wall. All I knew at the time was that I was leaving town to do a presentation at a conference, and this was going to ruin my new floors. Not once did I think about the mold that the water damage would cause. Not thinking about that aspect of things, eventually led to a status asthmaticus event when I returned from the conference. I had toxic mold growing in the walls of my condo and I didn't even know it. I began having more symptoms shortly after my return, but figured my triggers were just stress caused from pharmacy school, the recent end of a long-term relationship, in addition to the pressure to complete and present my research. Did I mention stress was one of my triggers? I still didn't think much of the water damage, and when I returned home from another experience where I was presenting our team's research, I realized my perspective on health and wellness was changing. My asthma symptoms were flaring up and focusing on my breathing was back on my radar. The white noise was becoming louder and louder. I was frustrated because I couldn't figure out what to do differently. I used breathing techniques, yoga, mindfulness, counseling, medication, and restricted my environment, but nothing wasn't working. None of it was enough.

I started to become flooded with fear, asking myself familiar questions like, "What if it was back? What if the white noise of constantly being focused on my breathing out of fear and helplessness, was going to take over once again? What if next time I really did die? What the hell is happening? Why was I losing the battle despite every intervention? Why now?" I was completely unaware that something in my seemingly very well controlled environment was the root of the cause and was literally growing worse every day while it was growing stronger. One evening I caught a glimpse of a dark shadow behind the armoire against my wall. When I couldn't figure out what it was, I pulled the armoire away from the wall. At that moment, it was like a slow-motion movie playing and I was in the lead role. Pulling the armoire away from the wall had released a huge plume of dark black spores into the air. I immediately panicked. I now knew why my asthma was getting worse. I had been living in a mold infested condo for months! That is what led to my uncontrolled inflammation, lung impairment, and eventually a nearly catastrophic event.

It was the first time I almost died over the age of thirty. I mean, that's such a bizarre thing to say, right? There were a few times as a child I was close to death, and I also had some other non-asthma related major health issues in my early twenties that I definitely shouldn't have lived through but did. However, not being in control of my asthma after devoting my life to making drastic lifestyle changes, was unexpected and concerning. It was determined I had to leave my condo and not return. It was a hazmat zone, so now I was in the hospital and was basically homeless. While in the hospital, I had a major adverse reaction to a medication I had been given for my lungs. It seemed like it was just my time. My prayer request had ended, and I was going to die. But, spoiler alert, I didn't. I decided I needed a new scripture to focus on, so I decided on Psalm 107:20 which reads, "He sent out his word and healed them, snatching them from the door of death." I started to make strides. I was taking insulin for the erratic glucose levels resulting from the insane amount of IV steroids I was on, just to keep my lungs open. I was giving myself my own insulin shots, taking my glucose levels, and notifying the nurses before and after meals. Did I have asthma and diabetes now? I learned the insulin was temporary until the IV meds would transition to oral, and then eventually inhalers, and things would calm down. I still had to check my glucose and report back, though. We would take it one day at a time, and that was fine with me. Every morning I woke up, I was just glad to have that day. I was *alive*.

Needless to say, post discharge, I could hardly function and was certainly not capable of functioning on my own. Not having the ability to return to my condo yet, and basically being homeless, was obviously a new challenge and new stressor. Who needs to experience all of this while in pharmacy school? Apparently, I did. I moved in with my classmate and best friend and her husband. One night, they were having a conversation about what would happen if I died in their house. They weren't trying to be rude, and it wasn't a negative conversation or them complaining. It was true, and at that time a realistic possibility. Honestly, I had the same question. Damn that white noise, I could hardly go up half a flight of stairs. It would take me nearly twenty minutes just to go up 7 steps. I would then sit in the stairwell landing where the stairs turned. Finally, after catching my breath, I would commit to getting up the next 7 stairs and crawling across the hall to my bed, no matter what. It was over a month before I was able to walk those stairs more normally, and it would be another month before I could return home by myself. It was months before my lungs could handle much of anything.

I started to do more research because there had to be something that I could use to help me gain control over my now hypersensitized airway so that I could actually return to school and return to my life. Something did start to change. Welcome to the world of wearing masks as a built-in buffer for indoor and outdoor triggers. At this point, I was on so many medications that I was quite literally feeling toxic. I had no appetite, my face looked gaunt, and my skin was yellowing. I was becoming toxic and had no idea what to do next. I began looking into what would help me cleanse my body of the toxins and rid the build-up and excess medications that were causing this new set of symptoms. My body was under a second wave of assault, and I felt helpless. I don't hate a lot of things, but I hate feeling helpless. It was imperative that I regained control, healed from the damage, and then dealt with the long-term consequences of the lung injury. I had to turn to God and trust there was a path toward healing because I was re-adopting the sick mentality and that was not where I wanted to be emotionally, mentally, spiritually, or physically.

I started to learn how the food I ate impacted my whole health. Then, I learned how my whole mind, body and spiritual health affected my breathing. An inflammatory diet contributed to the inflammatory processes and was connected to aeroallergens and environmental triggers, both indoor and outdoor. The inflammation was all having a negative impact in my life. I was slowly learning, slowly adapting, and slowly trying to understand, but was still not consistently eating an anti-inflammatory diet. That was a mental shift that I just didn't have in me. Not yet. I reviewed my medications and made sure I was optimized (optimized meaning I was on as few as possible to still breathe functionally and control inflammation) and working very openly with my provider at the university. He listened to me, asked me questions, asked me what I wanted to do, and helped me to identify what my goals were. I was so blown away. This was the best physician I ever had and the only one who sat with me to have a conversation first and then decide what approaches to take. He was partnering with me to shift my health, and this was going to change my life. I also had an amazing pulmonologist who really wanted to clear the slate and build something strong rather than just adding on more medications. These interactions finally aided my recovery and I felt like there was a different life ahead for me. This was how it should always be between a patient and their providers! I was on my way back to health. I was on my way back to healing, so very slowly, but I was making progress.

In 2008, I began teaching at a pharmacy school during my residency and have been in academia since. I have lectured and presented during grand rounds in doctorate programs in pharmacy, osteopathic medicine, physical therapy, optometry, and nursing. I began falling in love with pharmacology and approaches of clinical management for asthma and chronic obstructive pulmonary disease (COPD) and was exploring impacts from environmental triggers, lifestyle, and anti-inflammatory foods. I wanted more education for myself, so in turn I could offer more for my patients. I joined the state and local asthma coalitions and continue to serve in their leadership. I contributed to the development of strategic plans with a team of interprofessional colleagues with the Florida Asthma Coalition. I am constantly identifying avenues and opportunities to implement clinical and educational programs and services I have developed, or where I can contribute to the optimization of validated program components. I was breathing and I was thriving! I was building my recognition as a key contributor and identifying my place in the asthma practice community, within pharmacy, and in patient care management.

I moved to another area of the state (west coast) with the opportunity to work in a unique respiratory setting and environment. I was going to the only county in the state (at that time) with an air quality rating of F (think of grades in school, Fs are bad). I anticipated this would be an opportunity where I could potentially impact others, and I was determined to make a difference. I was feeling empowered and passionate, but still imprisoned because I realized I could not have complete control of my physical environment and there could be risks for my own health status. That transition proved to be fruitful because I partnered with a pediatric pulmonologist and pediatrician to work directly in their clinics and with their teams to impact patient outcomes. The physical environment where I was employed created major health challenges that would again require me to take a 360-degree approach and prepare for a spiritual, emotional, and physical battle. I was in a sick building, in a county with poor air quality, and over a period of two years, I had twenty-seven episodes ranging in severity completely due to my environment (indoor was the most significant driver).

I even experienced another nearly catastrophic event because of an exposure to a hazardous chemical on the floor in the hallway of my office building. The area was not blocked off, not properly ventilated, noticed with signage, or communicated with anyone (especially me) to give the opportunity to completely avoid the area, preventing injury or exacerbation. I remember it vividly and so do my students. I was walking down the hall to my classroom and ended up walking into this wall and a cloud of fumes that immediately sent my airway into spasm. I was wheezing, gasping, and recognized that I was in absolute crisis, and was fully aware that I could suffocate and die before getting down the stairwell, out the door, and into fresh air. I grabbed my inhaler out of my purse and tried to find any place I could go to get out of the fumes. I headed for the stairwell on the corner, only to be swarmed by another blast in the stairwell, which was also not ventilated. I ran in another direction to find another way out and immediately began praying, "I don't want to die. Not here. Not right now. Please!" I found a stairwell and made it down a flight of stairs, the inhaler wasn't helping, and the damage had clearly been done. I was not going to be able to manage this, reverse this, and I needed emergency help.

I started to panic. I struggled my way to my classroom where I wrote a note and left it with a student announcing that I was going to the emergency department, and I would record the lecture and follow up with the class later. By their faces, I already knew the students could see I was in crisis. I texted a colleague working at the closest hospital where I could access the emergency department, telling her I was coming in, and my lung status was dire. I asked her to please tell intake I was driving myself because there was no way an EMT would be able to find the building I was in, with the right entry point, and get me to the ED. I had two students help me get to my car. I accepted the reality that I may not actually make it and made peace with that. I drove down the street along the right shoulder for about 200 feet to the emergency department across the street. At the very least, I knew that if I didn't make it, I wouldn't cause an accident. I left my car running in the circle drive and struggled to make it the last 30 feet to get inside the front door.

I was determined not to die that day, but I was absolutely in a battle where the outcome was not in my control. I had surrendered in prayer and prayed over the team that was rushing to help stabilize me. Later that evening, when I had stabilized, I texted two friends and asked them for help getting me and my vehicle home. I reported the incident, filed for the absence, and got information on the chemical exposure (level 4 respiratory hazard). I found a new pulmonologist, who turned out to be my guardian angel. He was my champion through the challenges of reporting an exposure-related incident and assisted with activating medical leave. I could not talk because of the trauma to my airway, and my breathing was extremely laborious. We made major changes to my treatment, inclusive of my wishes for an integrated clinical approach. I was sad because I couldn't talk for over a month and had to incorporate yet another specialist in my care team for speech and swallowing. Months later, when I could talk and lecture again, I noticed my voice was different. It was hoarse, it was easily strained, and having a hyperactive airway made sensitivities to aeroallergens even more challenging in the environment I was in. I was sad, angry, and frustrated. But I was resilient, and I refused to let this overcome me. I decided I would use this new voice to make sure my story didn't become anyone else's story. I was determined to serve as an agent of that change.

I have been in organizational leadership within pharmacy, asthma, and public health, for over 17 years and I continue to seek out nontraditional training opportunities. It is important for me that I am able to demonstrate to my patients, colleagues, and the rest of my care teams the 360-degree approach and skill sets I bring in order to help identify, stage, manage, educate, treat, prevent, and control asthma. I was acutely aware how clinically significant the environment was, and I was going to make that part of every patient's treatment plan. I was learning how to become in tune with the physiology of my body through therapy. If I could align with the physiology, then I could surely realign the pathophysiology. Hello functional medicine! "Hello…. My friend…. Hello…." (You can always find a place for Neil Diamond). I was incorporating functional medicine into my own journey of healing this whole time, and I just didn't know how significant it could be with incredible outcomes. Now I harness the opportunities and approaches with great respect and admiration.

If my breathing went off course, I stepped in front of it and brought it back on track. I listened to my body and had control of my asthma instead of my asthma controlling me. I am fully aware of the slightest changes in my ability to breathe functionally. If the white noise was going to exist, it was going to exist on my terms. I am empowered by it. I can use it for good and to educate, just like a secret superpower. I was going to use my experiences to teach others, whoever they were, patients, students, families, and colleagues, being in tune with their breath is a very important part of their treatment. Now, I am able to gauge every inhalation and exhalation to determine if I'm having dysfunction or to self-assess for the level of my control. I have a full awareness of what my triggers are and how to mitigate them. I choose how to adjust and manage my asthma. Through functional medicine approaches and integrated clinical care, I was shifting my quality of life. My ability to experience a different life and my ability to breathe is finally within my control.

When I teach at the university to my pharmacy students in therapeutics, I share patient cases and experiences, asking them what they recognize, what they would target for management, and what they would recommend. I tell them about patients who were experiencing acute severe asthma (status asthmaticus) and misses by the healthcare team or institutions that leave patients at risk. There are some very emotional stories I share, and you can see in their faces and by their reactions they are listening, they are learning, and they will make better or different decisions for their patients. Eventually, I tell them which ones are actually experiences and my story. I believe the power of these patient cases and stories are serving as seeds planted in hundreds of student pharmacists who have since become practicing pharmacists. These pharmacists are now responsible for education, for shared decision-making, and are responsible for exploring every aspect of health with their patients. They can make decisions not just from a western medicine perspective, but from a whole health, functional medicine perspective as well. This change will be the difference between just treating the symptoms and actually helping patients to have lasting change in their health that they deserve.

I'm grateful that the passion I have for the treatment and management of asthma, is something personal, not just something I learned to manage out of interest. Because of the struggles I experienced, I can serve as a conduit for communication between the patient and their providers because I embody both. I am a patient. I am a provider. It's two different languages in the same conversation, and I can serve as a translator. I struggled more than necessary in my own health journey, and this is the story I want to share. I think about the breath cycle, inspiration, and expiration. Literally, the words inspiration and expiration are calling me to action. I am here to inspire change. Using traditional and integrative health management with my clinical team to reduce the burden that asthma has on an individual's life is how I choose to go to battle with asthma. There is a different life waiting on the other side of uncontrolled asthma for me and for my patients. I'm not an asthmatic. I am not asthma. I *have* asthma. I have taken control over my asthma, and I am here to empower and help others to do the same.

ABOUT DR. ANGELA S. GARCIA

Dr. Angela S. Garcia is trained and educated with a Bachelor of Psychology, Master of Public Health, and Doctorate of Pharmacy. Dr. Garcia is currently practicing as a clinical pharmacist, specializing in asthma management strategies and social determinants of health. Dr. Garcia has spent ten years in mental health facilities, almost ten years in population health, and close to fifteen years in a pharmacy practice where she integrates the knowledge from her three degrees, into a comprehensive model of care for optimized patient outcomes. She is residency trained in drug information, a licensed consulting pharmacist, and is certified in immunizations, Medication Therapy Management, Point of Care Testing, Spirometry, and Tobacco Treatment. Dr. Garcia has received numerous clinical, teaching, and service awards. She is a Certified Functional Medicine Specialist™ from Functional Medicine Business Academy™ and a Board Certified in Asthma Education.

Dr. Garcia is CEO and Founder of *AS Garcia Consulting Inc.*, which provides consulting services to ambulatory surgical centers and clinical consultations for complex patients with asthma and allergies. She is an accomplished author, program development interventionist, and skilled project coordinator. Her work has been featured and published in book chapters, biomedical journals, documentaries, news media, and developed various institutional programs, policies, and standard operating procedures. Dr. Garcia has substantial experience in program development and community grantsmanship, addressing social determinants and environmental health impacts in underserved populations.

Dr. Garcia authored the strategic plan for the Asthma Friendly Pharmacy Recognition program with the Florida Asthma Coalition and now serves on their steering committee. She held leadership positions in local, state, and national pharmacy and public health organizations, including serving as past president and chairman of the board for the Florida Pharmacy Association, member-at-large for the Florida Public Health Association, and currently sits on several committees to fulfill her passion to serve the needs of others.

Dr. Garcia's own journey of healing from medical and physical traumas has inspired her approach to integrate environmental health assessments. She is optimizing anti-inflammatory approaches to chronic disease management, healing through prayer and spirituality, and partners with regenerative health practitioners to return the body's homeostasis and maximize its capacity for healing. Identifying symptomatology as a result of negative effects from adverse emotional experiences and traumas, mismanaged stress, and the inflammatory process has always been a goal for Dr. Garcia. This approach opens the door for a healing breakthrough beyond what typical management with medications or invasive surgeries could offer.

After Dr. Garcia's own terrifying struggle with her inflammatory and allergy driven asthma, she has gained a greater understanding of the heterogeneous nature of asthma as a syndrome. She now works to identify management strategies through shared decision-making with her patients and clients in order to shift the dynamic and approach to care outcomes for those diagnosed with asthma. She is dedicated to using various medical approaches and practitioners to achieve optimized clinical outcomes around quality-of-life measures. She continues to work in undeserved and desperate communities to impact other's well-being through disease prevention and health promotion initiatives, as well as serves as an ambassador and champion for her patient's complex, health-related needs.

www.asthmafm.com | asgarciapharmd@gmail.com

Chapter 4

BORN FOR SOMETHING MORE

By Ani Rostomyan, PharmD, BCPS, APh

"If you always do what you've always done, you'll always get what you've always got."
– HENRY FORD

"Mom, you're such a nerd, but I'm super-duper proud of you." These were the words from the mouth of my young son as we were standing and hugging in the hallway of our California home, after I had received my doctorate diploma in the mail. I had just graduated as a Doctor of Pharmacy and received my diploma by mail from Massachusetts College of Pharmacy and Health Sciences. I remember it well. It was a sunny September afternoon in 2017, and that day brought me my second diploma in higher education. I officially became a Doctor of Pharmacy at 35 years old, while also navigating the challenges that came along with being a single mother in a full-time clinical position and had recently relocated to California. At this moment, I gave the diploma to my son and told him, "Garik, I want you to remember, the sky's the limit, and you can achieve anything you want in life, if you have your mind set on it."

My 9-year-old sunshine looked at me with his eyes wide open, and I saw that he believed every single word I uttered at that moment. He, like no one else, knew the price of that diploma. Any available spare time we had together we went to parks, museums, and extracurricular activities, but motherly guilt was my best friend through those years. My favorite human on earth, my munchkin, knew that his mom was on a mission, and she had to finish school. Kids have tremendous coping skills we adults sometimes lack.

Being an immigrant from Armenia and having achieved so much in just a decade of moving and adapting to life in the United States, you would think it would give me an immense amount of career satisfaction and self-confidence. But boy was I wrong, and in so many ways. My overachieving anxious mind told me, "I'm not happy, not confident, not fulfilled. I just know something is off." Obviously, something was off if I still wasn't satisfied after completing two degrees and working in my career as I had intended.

I grew up in a small town in the ancient country of Armenia, a tiny Republic of the former Soviet Union. Although my country is small, it has a history dating back to the cradle of civilization. We lost our lands and sovereignty throughout the centuries, because of our faith, and now are left with only 11,484 sq. miles of our beloved Motherland. Armenia is the first nation on Earth that accepted Christianity as its official religion, and the country is a museum under the sky with its early Christian churches and pre-Christian era pagan temples. Both my parents were children of immigrants, repatriated from Iran to the land of their ancestors in the early 1940s and 1960s. The town where I grew up was 20 minutes away from the capital, Yerevan, which is comfortably located in between mountains and canyons, where the air is crisp and clean and the water is crystal clear, the best in the world.

In my hometown, everyone knew each other and lived close by. My mother was a Russian language teacher in one of the elementary schools, and my father was the town dentist, a maxillofacial surgeon, and a well-known doctor in the area. We were truly a picture-perfect family: great parents, three daughters who were all excellent students, modest and proper, as we were meant to be in our culture.

For me, going to medical school and continuing in my father's footsteps, was a no-brainer. My oldest sister and I chose medical school, and my middle sister, who was more of a foreign language and history geek, chose diplomacy and international relations. We were our parents' pride and joy. My father was very involved in our education and career choices. He decided that instead of dental school, I should attend pharmacy school, a more appropriate choice for a woman, so I could have a better work-life balance. I couldn't be happier now to have chosen Pharmacy as my profession, but back then, I was left feeling like my parents were making decisions for me, instead of me choosing who I wanted to become. My entire life was designed around following what my parents told me to do, until my mid-20s, when my soul rebelled, and it told me to follow my *dream*, to follow my *joy*.

In the early 2000s, my father was diagnosed with Type-2 Diabetes, which runs on his side of the family. When we found out about his diabetes diagnosis in 2000, our world crashed with him. I was a pharmacy student at the time and did not have enough knowledge and expertise to know how much of an impact nutrition has on diabetic patients. We were trying our best, however, to figure out ways to help him with diet and medications. My father was not a good patient, despite being a great doctor himself. He was in denial, claiming that once you have the disease, there's not much you can do. He decided not to worry about what would happen next.

Over the years, I witnessed how his diabetes progressed. He experienced the classic complications of constantly having elevated blood sugar. His vision and kidney function declined, peripheral neuropathy (the result of damage to the nerves located outside his brain and spinal cord) surfaced with sharp burning pain in his feet, making his quality of life unbearable. He adamantly refused insulin and other medications and wasn't following his recommended diet. He was caving to his disease, even though there was treatment available to him.

Fast-forward a few years later, he was finally ready to make changes and start tackling his disease, but his complications had progressed, and there was little we could do. Diabetes is a silent killer, and oftentimes symptoms don't alarm patients until organ damage has taken place, when it may be too late to reverse detrimental consequences. This was the case for my dad. He unfortunately waited too long to take his health seriously, and this decision led to his early death which shook our family to the core.

In 2010, he passed away from stroke and diabetes complications, at the young age of 69. We were visiting Armenia with my 10-month-old son, to baptize him and spend time with our family. Within a week after we returned to the United States, he had a stroke and became bedridden, until the day he departed this earth. That was the only time he was able to spend time with my son who, unlike other grandchildren, looks just like him. With my almost 1-year-old son, I was unable to fly back to attend his funeral which left a hole in my heart forever.

After my father's loss, I made a pledge to myself to learn as much as I could about diabetes prevention and management, so I could help as many patients as I possibly could. This is the very first time I've ever shared this, but I see my father in every diabetes patient who says he or she does not have time to take care of their health, and that there are other priorities, such as family, work and bills. I want to hold their hand and say that later is now. There is no better time to make the changes. Tomorrow may be too late, just like it was for my dad.

As healthcare professionals, empathy is a quality most of us naturally embody. We feel our patient's worries and struggles, understand their socioeconomic and health barriers, as well as the hardships they face daily. Sometimes, we must be the bearers of bad news, explaining to our patients the harsh reality and the detrimental consequences of their unmanaged disease.

Moving to the United States in 2007, at the age of 25, was not an easy venture. I had a mission to relearn many things, including English. I wanted to adopt new cultural traditions and reestablish myself as a professional. The first year of my life in the United States was filled with all sorts of struggles like homesickness, language barriers, and cultural adaptation. Many times, in public, I would get "stuck," unable to explain myself at the grocery store or mispronouncing words. Later, I had nightmares about it, which made me decide to take charge of my accent and improve my English first.

The insecurity of being an immigrant stays with you. I always aspired to overachieve and prove myself in my own eyes to look equal to others. I felt the need to prove that I was a good fit in this society. My dream was to become an exceptional Pharmacist in the US, which led to my decision to pursue another Pharmacy degree while working incredibly long hours as a full-time Pharmacist for a well-known retail chain.

Seven years to the day that I moved to the US, I found myself as a single mom, with new realities, a new job, in a new state, and was starting pharmacy school again. Let me tell you, single motherhood is no picnic. You are the mom, dad, friend, caregiver, and the disciplinarian, all-in-one. Looking back at the years when I had to quickly make life changes and be brave, not necessarily by choice, I realize these years helped me in so many ways. They helped to build a strong confidence and pride in myself.

Years later, I met with a friend, and she shared about going through hardships as a single parent. I cheered her on by saying, "Girl, you don't have a clue how strong you are. There is always sunshine after rain, always, that's the rule of life." I can honestly say that I handled single motherhood as well as possible. The introverted and shy girl grew up to be a fierce woman, who moved across the country, and applied and accepted a highly paid Pharmacist position. With English as my second language, I relied on a strong work ethic and a lot of determination, and I did it. My determination to excel and learn was so much stronger than my physical and mental abilities at the time, but I dove into the journey anyway.

On the weekends and varying weeks, I flew back and forth to Boston for school. I worked endless shifts, juggled single parenthood, and it was an astonishing life lesson. Burnout became my new norm, and it was tolerable, but I was also scared. Being a single mom at the time and the only income earner induced panicked thoughts of losing my job. At the same time, the overpowering feeling of financial instability kept me going. My mind questioned whether this was going to be my reality for the rest of my career. At that time, I was purely relying on my pride to complete whatever I started, since my mental and physical energy were absolutely depleted. I soon moved to a more clinical setting and fulfilled my dream of becoming a pharmacist who provides direct care to patients and manages chronic disease states, in addition to dispensing medications and counseling patients. My dream was coming true. I was going to be getting an incredible opportunity to help patients with diabetes, a rewarding and challenging journey for a clinical pharmacist.

The realities of conventional medicine are sadly less promising. There's very little provider-patient one-on-one time and instead, there's more paperwork and healthcare logistical issues. I wish we could go back in time one thousand years to be the healers of medicine, not having to resolve insurance and paperwork issues at all. Yes, I like to dream... My frustration grew as I saw patients who were not getting better with the conventional medical approach. With the diabetes treatment options available nowadays, our healthcare statistics should certainly show declining incidence, not vice-versa. Yet, we see it becoming more prevalent in younger people, affecting teenagers now.

My father's health issues resurfaced daily while having interactions with my patients, which convinced me that more medications didn't mean better healthcare. Instead, lifestyle changes are the key. Doctors and pharmacists are helpless if our patients don't make core lifestyle changes in managing diabetes and alter their approach to food. I realized that as a pharmacist, I'm uniquely positioned to manage diabetes with medication and nutrition knowledge, leading me to look for a better solution. The answer is to accept food as a medicine and spread that knowledge and empowerment to people needing my help.

My attitude to life comes from my mother, an extraordinarily optimistic woman, educator, and psychologist. She always reminds me, "Ani, remember, if water is spilled on the ground, it always finds its way to spread around. Don't worry, your dreams will materialize." Speaking to so many influential women, throughout and after 2020, has taught me one invaluable lesson- everyone has their own story and hardships. No one's life is perfect, and they all are the authors of their own book of life.

They are in charge of rewriting the chapter if they don't like the previous one.

2020 taught me to collect memories, not things. I gained more friendships and met more influential people, both in my field and outside my field, than ever before in my adult life. I started networking, listening to other people's success stories, and reading far more about leadership and personal transformation journeys than ever before. My entrepreneurial side also comes from my mother. She is a risk-taker and inspiration. She always encourages me to chase my dreams, where my father always taught me to follow orders, be a good employee, play in the safe zone, and to never take risks. The simplicity and, at the same time, complexity of making a life-changing decision coexist together. You meet people who can make drastic career and life changes, alter their mindset, embrace new beginnings, and simply thrust themselves into it. However, you find it extremely hard to implement it for yourself.

Fear, that nasty, negative word, my least favorite word of all time. Fear knows you're fearing it. It knows when to come to you and when to occupy your mind. Thoughts tend to materialize in the most unique way. The more we think and concentrate on the negative, the more it becomes incredibly imprinted in our nature. The bottom line, and why I decided to write my story for myself as much as for others, is to reinforce my commitment to starting new ventures and learning new approaches. What is the worst that can happen if you don't succeed in your endeavors? You can always go back to your 9-5 job and continue your career, but can you succeed if you don't try? As Wayne Gretzky has said, "We always miss 100% of the shots we don't take." So, in short, the answer is NO!

It is human nature to strive for better. During my journey over the past year, I learned about brain-gut connection, root causes of chronic disease, and biochemical pathways interlinked in our bodies. I had never been exposed to these concepts before. I have always been taught that allopathic medicine was the only way to go. But now here I am, learning about integrative, functional medicine, and even more recently, about pharmacogenomic variations in our genome, which greatly affect our drug and nutrient metabolism. The 'aha' moment is striking me every day.

Will there ever be a period in my lifetime where all of this becomes standard patient care? Will conventional medical and pharmacy schools start teaching about integrative approach and how to prevent disease rather than over medicate our society? My nerdy personality quickly pulled me back to studying and learning more about how a holistic approach and de-prescribing, can often be the best way to care for your patient, along with a traditional approach.

Ideally, all these approaches of medicine should be implemented hand-in-hand. Not curing just the disease but healing the patient as a whole. Utilizing an integrative approach in standard care can truly lead to wonders. The US healthcare system is very strong in providing acute care, saving us from bacterial and viral infections, stroke complications, heart attacks and other life-threatening conditions. Preventative and chronic disease management, on the other hand, relies on the patient's motivation and mindset. It's so easy to fall into the trap of the fast-food industry, avoid cooking and shopping time, and become part of the brainwashed, dopamine-craving, and dependent reward system. Millions of Americans use fast, calorie-rich food to fill the void in their life. The same void that can be filled with meditation, cooking healthy meals, walks in the park and learning about food history and sharing meals together.

Working with diabetes patients and learning more about management of the root cause of chronic disease, I realized that Type-2 diabetes is almost completely preventable. With implementation of lifestyle management and working on changing lifelong habits, with healthy alternatives, not short-term fad diet-style change.

Being an introverted person and trying to use social media to position myself in various platforms as a professional, to this day, are my biggest struggles. I remember recording a 15-second video repeatedly, and each time I was consumed with the same thoughts. "I hate my voice. I hate my choice of words. I don't like how I look. I'm not credible. Who would like me? I have a weird accent; people won't listen to me. Why would someone follow my advice?" My entire day would be spent recording myself for 15 seconds of a health topic, before I would crash, hopelessly.

Many times, in elementary school, I knew the answer to my teacher's questions, and my shy nature wouldn't allow me to speak up or raise my hand. My entire day would be ruined because of that. I bashed myself and criticized myself, saying, "Why didn't I just raise my hand? Why couldn't I just be bold and brave?"

Working as a retail pharmacist in a well-known chain was beyond an eye-opening experience to how much more I could multitask as a pharmacist and how highly unappreciated our profession truly is to our employers. Feeling guilty for incomplete tasks was definitely experienced more often than giving myself a nice tap on the back and saying, "Good job, girl! You handled so much today."

During my time living in South Florida, I became a registered pharmacist and it taught me incredibly valuable life lessons. There were days when my only choice was to stay as strong as possible and keep moving forward. I was always taught that a small, steady income is always better than risky business endeavors. Starting a business is not for women, and women should always have low stress, low risk jobs to dedicate more of their time to the family and raising kids. That's the programming that worked in Armenian society, and women tend to accept that reality even nowadays and kill the dreams they had for entrepreneurship. Because of my programming from childhood, I tended to explain myself constantly, apologize needlessly, or always feel guilty. I never advocated for myself. Throughout much of my conscious living, I was taught to be a follower and excel at what I do for others' benefit. I was never taught to value myself, negotiate my salary, my terms, or stand up for myself.

Reading more and listening to more podcasts, mostly on personal development, I came across a podcast episode about imposter syndrome. Even the most famous and successful entrepreneurs and celebrities suffer from it. A successful Hollywood "A" star actress, businesswoman, and founder of the "Honest Company", Jessica Alba, confessed to suffering from imposter syndrome, doubting herself and questioning why she is getting paid so much and is she even talented? In her words, she would think, "It was God, magic, or just pure luck" that brought her success and entrepreneurial accomplishments, but not her own hard work and determination. I felt so connected to her. There I was, an imposter victim.

Growing up, I realized that I could manage my introverted personality on public platforms if I could speak about things that provide me joy and that are in line with my passions and, voila! I saw a mindset shift happening. Little did I know that mindfulness practice, meditation, and non-judgmental awareness of my anxiety would help me get over the fears. We can overcome uncomfortable social experiences if we embrace the attitude that everything will be alright at the end, as well as visualize a successful outcome. After sharing a video of my healthy recipe one day, a friend thanked me for it, as she found it helpful and was looking forward to more tips on how to manage her diabetes. With that mindset, I felt a little more encouraged and motivated, rather than being dismissive of it. Counseling patients in a work setting was my daily routine as a pharmacist but sharing it on social platforms was so new to me.

Talking to my dear friend, colleague, and mentor Dr. Christine Manukyan, who shifted her career from hospital clinical pharmacist to functional medicine business coach, was enlightening to me. The harsh belief that we, as pharmacists, are stuck in a model of only a few practice options, was thankfully broken. I felt unstuck and enlightened. Unstuck is one of my favorite words now. For the first time in my life and career as a healthcare professional, I felt liberated and in charge.

My biggest passion is learning new concepts, new theories, emerging scientific evidence and teaching it to others. As Leonardo Da Vinci said, "Learning never exhausts the mind." I started manifesting and visualizing the patient-centered, holistic business I was soon to be establishing and I knew that my motivation was not merely my end goal, but more about eagerness of reaching the goal.

2020 was a tough journey, I learned a lot, made mistakes, and moved on. I am so thankful to some extent for the pandemic year for my own personal transformation. What I also realized is the extraordinary transformation journey you start as a professional should not be painful and exhausting. The journey or adventure should make you enjoy the process and wait for final results. Invaluable in its own respects was finding a tribe of like-minded women who uplift each other, rather than bring each other down, and who cheer and support each other over competing against the other.

Looking back at the person I was twenty years ago, I went through a rather impressive transformation. Never in my wildest dreams did I imagine becoming a business owner and health practitioner that changes people's lives. Nor did I imagine I'd be a person who strives to learn more every day. My old self was drowning in negative self-talk, filtering out the good and only thinking about what I didn't accomplish. I was focusing on everything negative happening around me and taking the blame for it. I would catastrophize or polarize events, either anticipating the worst or expecting things not to go my way.

Little did I know, negative thoughts can physically affect us. They are exhausting and keep you stuck in a place where you can't see anything positive happening. I still have moments in the evening when some troubling thoughts surface in my consciousness. As a transformed person, I meditate and observe the feelings from above, not allowing the negative thoughts to linger. I want to give myself the best compliment now. These are my personal wins, my personal growth, learning how to acknowledge my value, building a support group, becoming more adaptable and just starting literally from small changes. The question I ask myself now is not whether I *can* do it. Rather, I ask *how* I will do it?

ABOUT DR. ANI ROSTOMYAN

Dr. Ani Rostomyan is a board-certified Ambulatory Care Clinical Pharmacist who specializes in Diabetes management and Pharmacogenomics consulting. Dr. Ani received her master's degree in Pharmacy through Yerevan State Medical University in Armenia in 2005. Dr. Ani Rostomyan later earned her doctorate degree in Pharmacy in 2017 from Massachusetts College of Pharmacy and Health Sciences, Boston, MA. Dr. Ani has been practicing in an Ambulatory Care setting as a Clinical Pharmacist in Los Angeles, CA for the last 7 years.

Dr. Ani's greatest passion through her pharmacist career is in helping and coaching patients with Type 2 Diabetes, who have low health literacy and medication non-compliance, and educating them how to use food as medicine. Dr. Ani has transformed hundreds of patients' lives and helped them achieve outstanding results in diabetes control, weight loss, and a more positive mindset about their health. Having helped countless patients as a Clinical Pharmacist, she made the decision to start her own functional wellness practice in order to serve more people in their health transformation journey through the use of personalized medicine as part of their care.

Dr. Ani discovered her calling in Precision Medicine as well, quickly becoming a certified Pharmacogenomics and Nutrigenomics trained Pharmacist, and a consultant. Dr. Ani firmly believes that diabetes is not only managed through traditional doctor's offices, but is, in fact, primarily prevented and managed in our very own kitchens and pantries. Culinary and lifestyle choices are the beginning of ending most chronic diseases that are sadly becoming a healthcare Epidemic of the 21st century.

Dr. Ani Rostomyan is the founder of *SheAni, Inc*, a concierge consulting company, focused on providing diabetes coaching as well as Pharmacogenomic and Nutrigenomic consulting services to patients. Her practice is fully focused on functional and holistic ways of improving overall health and well-being.

Dr. Ani is on a mission to empower other Pharmacists to believe in themselves, just as she has done, and to never be afraid of moving beyond their comfort zone. She is spreading the message to never let your fears hold you back from achieving your greatest potential.

dranirostomyan.com | rxhealthcoaching@gmail.com | IG: @dr.anirotomyan

Chapter 5

FROM UNHEARD STRUGGLES TO RECLAIMING FREEDOM: A MOM'S JOURNEY TO REAL ANSWERS

By Areeman Saed, PharmD

"Only one who devotes himself to a cause with his whole strength and soul can be a true master. For this reason, mastery demands all of a person."
– ALBERT EINSTEIN

"I can't walk. I can't walk," screamed my daughter at the Istanbul airport, as she collapsed down on the floor. This happened on our way to Turkey and then Iraqi Kurdistan (my native country), on a summer vacation. It was supposed to be a fun and exciting time for my family, taking them back home for the first time since they were infants. We landed in Istanbul airport and that's when my daughter started complaining of not being able to walk anymore. I thought it was just from exhaustion and walking from one side of the airport to the other side to get to our gate. I attended to her and started to wonder what could have caused such pain in her legs, to the point that she couldn't walk from the pain in her bones. I gave her some medicine (ibuprofen) to help alleviate the pain she was experiencing. After about an hour, she felt better, and we started heading over to our gate for our next flight. I was happy to see her smile and be able to walk again, but deep down inside me, the questions were running wild in my mind. What could have caused this? What could be wrong with my child? We contacted a friend who is a pediatrician to get some input regarding this incident. She reassured us that it could be growing pains, and there was nothing to be concerned about.

This incident made me think of the time when she was three and half years old, refused to walk, and was crawling around the house. A child complaining of leg pain or refusing to walk is a natural concern to parents. She started crying because she couldn't walk up the stairs and continued to avoid putting pressure on her feet. Even though she was a toddler and had been walking for two years, we had to carry her all the time in those days. The doctor told us at that time it was due to viral myositis. A benign, acute childhood myositis is a mild and self-limiting condition of sudden onset lower extremity pain during or following recovery from a viral illness. I managed her pain with over-the-counter analgesics, and she was back to full energy after a couple of days.

After we got back from our vacation, I started doing some research and wasn't satisfied with the simple answer of "it's just growing pains." I asked for extensive lab work from her pediatrician, labs that they normally don't check. My daughter hates to be poked. She was crying so much and asking why they needed to take so much blood, and I had to fight my emotions and continue the line-up of blood work and testing. A few days later, I received a phone call from the doctor's office. The nurse informed me that all her blood work came back normal, except for her vitamin D levels. She mentioned that her vitamin D was extremely low, and she needed to be on supplements daily.

In western medicine, and during regular checkups, checking vitamin D is not a routine thing. Vitamin D is one of many vitamins our bodies need to stay healthy. It has many functions, including maintaining strong and healthy bones. Weak bones can lead to osteoporosis. A vitamin D deficiency may also be linked to a higher risk of depression, and that's why they call vitamin D a "sunshine vitamin." You can get most of your vitamin D from exposure to the sun for 15-20 minutes on a daily basis. However, in some cases, you need additional supplementation to get the optimal level.

I was happy to find the answers that we had been looking for, but at the same time, I started to wonder how many similar cases go unnoticed, with so many possible long-term implications. As a parent, it made me question our way of handling daily issues pertaining to our children's health. How often could this be mistaken or automatically judged for other conditions? I started wondering what could have been the cause of such low vitamin D in such a young child. Besides supplements, what else can we do to prevent this from happening? She was a perfectly healthy baby, and I remember I was told it was only a deficiency in vitamin D, and it could easily be fixed with over-the-counter supplements. As a healthcare professional myself, however, I know the complications of chronic low vitamin D are serious and we needed to bring her levels up before it damaged other parts of her body. This was an eye-opening experience for me and made me think deeply of my own struggle with fatigue and low energy for the previous 5-6 years.

During my third pregnancy, I developed severe nausea and vomiting, also known as hyperemesis gravidarum (HG). HG can lead to severe dehydration requiring hospitalization for fluid resuscitation, which ended up being the case for me. My previous two pregnancies were uneventful, so this presentation of symptoms was stressful for me. During my hospitalization, they hydrated me with IV fluids and treated my nausea and vomiting with antiemetics. After extensive lab work, including heart monitoring, they diagnosed me with hypothyroidism (or as we like to call it, "hypo"). I started treatment immediately and was given hope that I could get off the medication after the pregnancy. I trusted my doctors and took my medicines, however my TSH level was fluctuating to the point where I almost lost my baby to this awful disease, at just 15 weeks pregnant. I'm forever grateful and blessed to have been able to carry my baby to full-term, but I know there are a lot of other women out there that have lost or miscarried their babies due to complications from this condition.

Looking back, I realized that I had various symptoms of hypothyroidism, tracing back almost three years before the diagnosis. My doctors always assured me that I didn't have that condition, simply because my thyroid lab work always came back within the "normal" range or was just slightly off. It was very frustrating. I went from doctor to doctor who told me to try this diet and make this or that change. However, none of those recommendations helped my extreme fatigue, mood swings, brain fog, or my ability to control my weight fluctuations. I always felt like something was wrong inside my body.

Hypothyroidism may not cause noticeable symptoms in the early stages. However, untreated hypothyroidism can cause a number of health problems, some potentially serious. For years, I had increased fatigue, loss of energy, sensitivity to cold (especially in my hands and feet), hair loss, weight gain, a foggy brain, and itchy skin. I was told that all these conditions may simply be attributed to getting older or that it is just in my head, and that all my lab work tests were, again, normal. Getting old? That couldn't be the real answer.

I did fine with the rest of my pregnancy, and after the birth of my son, I was taken off my medication. I was told my TSH, T3, and T4 levels (the markers that they check to see if your body is producing enough thyroid hormone), were normal, and that I didn't need thyroid replacement anymore. I was happy to not take any medications anymore, however, my symptoms were back again within months of stopping the medication, and I felt worse than ever. I went back to my doctor and started back on the medications, but this time, getting back on them didn't alleviate my symptoms right away, like it had when I was pregnant. One thing I learned while battling the treatment for my hypothyroidism is don't just accept, "You are fine," from your doctor. Ask for specific lab results and optimal ranges for each of the results.

The brain fog that you have to fight on a daily basis, because you can't remember the name of the person you worked with previously, or your kids' appointments, isn't normal. Imagine if you couldn't remember a word that describes your illness, and you go home to do research in google and have no idea where to start. Imagine walking to your garage looking for something and forgetting once you get out there why you went out there in the first place. This was my reality.

I felt like a walking zombie. I was tired, grumpy, and constantly fighting weight fluctuations. In the face of the coronavirus pandemic, and the uncertainty it has brought to our lives, I reached my breaking point. I was just tired and exhausted all the time. Getting out of bed felt grueling and punishing. This wasn't about the virus, per se, nor was it about the stress of being confined at home. This was about a tiny butterfly gland that is located in the back of my neck that was not working properly and causing me to experience all these problems in my body. Taking one small pill for it just wasn't working anymore.

It is very painful to describe how all of this affected my heart, mind, and soul, in general. It had changed me into a person I couldn't even recognize anymore. I was always second guessing myself, and it affected my confidence and level of thinking. People who have gone through this will understand exactly what I'm saying. When you are hypo, everything is slowed down in your body, and sometimes, I felt as if I was slowly dying.

Roughly 16 million women will, at some point, have a breakdown of the thyroid. The thyroid produces hormones that touch every cell and help regulate our metabolism, our bowels, and our brains. Hypothyroidism, or an underactive thyroid, is a condition in which your thyroid gland doesn't produce enough of the important hormones. It is one of the most undiagnosed, misdiagnosed, and unrecognized health problems in the world nowadays. Hypothyroid patients are falling through the cracks of mainstream medicine, left to suffer debilitating, and even life-threatening, symptoms.

I decided to take control of my health and my life. After extensive research, I decided to treat my symptoms with lifestyle modifications and a dietary adjustment. The first thing I did to begin my new lifestyle was a pantry remodel. This meant I took out all the processed, unhealthy snacks and food. I gradually incorporated intermittent fasting into my life. There are many ways that people do IF, but the way it worked for me was to limit my eating to an approximately 8 hours window. This gave my body a chance to rest and repair and process the nutrients during the fasting hours. In addition, I tried to consume mostly organic fruits and vegetables and grass-fed meat. I cut out most of the food that causes inflammation, including processed red meat, refined grains, artificial food additives, etc. These foods contain ingredients that can trigger or worsen inflammation, and hence worsen the symptoms of hypothyroidism.

I stopped consuming sugar and grains and reduced my carbohydrate consumption. There is some evidence that a high carb diet may promote inflammation in some people, and based on that, I decided to limit it in my diet to see if I could see a difference in my symptoms. Coming from a culture that consumes a lot of rice, white bread, potatoes, and sweets, this was challenging for me at the beginning. However, I had a different mindset this time, and was determined to heal my body.

I hired a fitness coach to help me with weight loss. After the very hard work of adding different aerobic and anaerobic exercises, I was able to lose over 20lbs. I now have a lot more energy, and I am able to play with my kids, and enjoy spending time with my family. I don't struggle with memory issues like I did before. I don't wake up exhausted and tired, and I feel quite refreshed after adequate sleep. Improving sleep quality and getting better sleep may decrease the risk of developing chronic inflammation, which, in turn, will help you feel better. I'm slowly starting to become adjusted. I felt much better shortly after initiating thyroid replacement medicine, but it took me months to feel like I've regained that zest for life. I'm not one to talk publicly about my problems and issues, but this has affected me so much, and I know there are a lot of other women out there that are going through the exact same thing. If sharing my story helps even one person to find the willpower to heal their body naturally, then I am happy to be the voice of change for them.

To give you a bit of context as to how my journey in this country first began, I want to take you back to 1996, when my family was forced to be evacuated from Iraq to the United States, due to political unrest and safety concerns. Settling in a new country with seven children was a tall order for my parents. Their continuous sacrifices carried us through the challenges, uncertainties, and struggles. From the very beginning, I had interest in the healthcare field, and it was quite an adjustment to learn about the major areas of difference between the centralized and crippled healthcare system back home and the more open and highly developed one in this country. Nonetheless, as I went through pharmacy school and then stepped into the workforce, I came to realize there are still many areas where our US healthcare system can be improved and built on. One of the strongest points my immigrant background provided me is the ability to see through the eyes and experiences of the less fortunate, the underserved, and those who have poor access to healthcare. Furthermore, as I reflected deeper into our flawed vision of our own health system, I realized even those of us with adequate access to good healthcare still often overlook the depth of understanding of the importance of looking beyond just diagnosis and therapy dispensary. These discoveries through my story are what led me to the healthcare field in the first place.

I have been in the health field for over 13 years, from shadowing doctors, interning in a dental office, to finally settling to go to pharmacy school. I have always had an interest in healthcare. I loved this field because my passion was to make people feel better. I wanted to pursue my dreams of helping others, and pharmacy seemed like a good way to begin that journey towards accomplishing my dreams. The fast-paced nature of retail pharmacy proved to be challenging, however. The way it is set up to meet immediate demands, with very small chances to focus on the real solutions, was disheartening to me.

I worked in retail pharmacy in various roles, including management, for the beginning of my career, then transitioned into a clinical position at the hospital after I finished my residency. Working in retail didn't satisfy me as far as helping people with their personal health journey's. Working in retail pharmacy is like working on a production line in a factory. It is not even close to possible for high-volume pharmacies to meet the demands and expectations that are set for them by the corporate world.

The stress levels can be very hard on one's health as well. In addition to that, the highly technical demands take away from the ability of a provider to connect more closely with patients. You need to be able to multitask, while remaining focused on accuracy, during all steps of the order fulfillment process. We don't get enough time to spend with patients and explain to them how to take their medications properly, or to listen to their concerns to understand the full picture. The current structure of patient encounters hinders our ability, as providers, to spend time with patients that is adequate enough to provide a more comprehensive approach to assessment, planning and education.

I have always believed in holistic medicine because I believe good health is a combination of physical, mental, spiritual, and emotional well-being. After the pandemic started, I started to look for different methods to improve my own immune system, and that's when I came across the concept of functional medicine. I learned later, I had used the same concept, not knowingly, to improve my own symptoms from hypothyroidism. I researched more about functional medicine and came across many groups of women who are in this field and making a huge impact on their patients' lives. I wanted to learn even more and get the knowledge to empower myself to help myself first, and then people around me. My personal struggles with my own health, and my daughter's experience, and then my self-introduction to the world of functional medicine, have allowed me to further look into the struggles of other people around me, including my close family members.

My own battle of reclaiming my health, and my struggles with navigating the American healthcare system, as well as my daughter's struggles, have all brought me a sense of enlightenment. These struggles have made me think of the gap in our healthcare system. I didn't want to treat my poor focus, fatigue, itching, and my acid reflux with acid blockers, stimulants, and steroids, which is often considered to be the only available option towards healing. This is where the concept of functional medicine started to solidify in my mind.

We shouldn't be treating every problem with different pharmaceuticals that may cause other harmful side effects. I learned through functional medicine that you can treat the root cause of the problem, rather than patching it with bandages. In functional medicine, the practitioner will focus on multiple factors that could be the cause of certain problems including environmental, psychological, spiritual, and social factors, as well as genetic makeup. As I learned more about this, I decided to obtain my certificate in pharmacogenomics. This helps me to be able to see a specific person's genetic makeup and how it affects the medications they take. This personalized approach to medicine, where we eliminate the guesswork, can help determine whether a certain medication or dose will work for a patient, without causing side effects. Pharmacogenomics is a new concept, and more research is currently underway to fully understand the power and science behind how we can begin to practice medicine in a more direct and healing manner.

Reflecting on my journey, and the positive impact it ultimately had on me, I am now looking for ways to pass that positive impact on to others around me. Currently, being on track towards becoming a functional medicine specialist is the beginning of an exciting endeavor. Using my extensive training, knowledge, and personal experience, I have been equipped with a multitude of skills to help others who are going through challenging health-related circumstances. My involvement with a team of other professionals, and aspiring providers, all with one common interest in a new approach to understanding the body, and the delivery of the healing process, has added more to my excitement than I ever could have imagined.

My long-term plan includes incorporating functional medicine into my practice, as an already practicing clinical pharmacist. The training and experience will also give me a chance to take this thought and process into other medical practices, including my husband's multi-specialty clinic. Furthermore, I would like to create a platform to introduce this idea into our underserved communities and rural areas, where proper education is often lacking. I want to be part of positive change that will be long-lasting and healing to those that need it the most. It's never too late to start over again, so don't settle for a job or career that's not allowing you to maximize your impact.

ABOUT DR. AREEMAN SAED

Dr. Areeman Saed is a Certified Functional Medicine Specialist™ from Functional Medicine Business Academy™ and is a clinical pharmacist, specializing in antimicrobial stewardship, medication therapy management, and pharmacogenomic consulting. She has over 13 years of pharmacy experience, including various leadership roles in healthcare settings such as community, hospital, and academia. Dr. Saed has helped patients for more than a decade with optimizing their drug regimen, evaluating drug interactions to avoid patient harm, and recommending therapy changes to improve a patient's health.

Through Dr. Saed's personal journey of healing her own body and mind with lifestyle and dietary changes, she is driven towards exploring many disciplines in healthcare in order to broaden her clinical knowledge and incorporate it into her practice. Dr. Saed is passionate about working with people to offer the best choices in personalized medicine, through pharmacogenomic testing, functional medicine assessment, lifestyle modifications, and supplementation, to identify the root cause of the problem. She has a special interest in understanding cultural diversity in viewing the mind, body, health, and overall well-being. Through this understanding, she hopes to bring better clarity and care for those who are a part of under-served communities. She is a lifelong learner, constantly working to further expand her knowledge about holistic approaches to wellness.

Dr. Saed is on a mission to positively impact low-income communities through providing personalized, exemplary care. This care will not be determined by insurance coverage as traditional healthcare typically is, but rather, will be focused on the hearts and bodies of deserving people everywhere, no matter their socioeconomic status.

www.drareemansaed.com | drareemansaed@gmail.com | IG: @dr.areemansaed

Chapter 6

A NEW PERSPECTIVE YIELDS HOPE FOR CHANGE

By Brooke Spino, PharmD

"Regardless of the specific decisions we make throughout our lives, at the heart of each one is the chance to examine ourselves; to make changes that increase our sense of possibility and accomplishment; and to have a life of authenticity, purpose, and inspiration."
– Matt Walker, Adventure in Everything

Every single day, I speak with people who are desperate for answers. They are stuck in a perpetual game of ping pong, being bounced back and forth between various doctors who all seem to have different treatment advice for their chronic disease. Many of my patients and close friends have come to accept their fate of feeling unwell or just taking the medications their doctor has ordered in hopes of relieving their symptoms. It has become abundantly clear to me that there is a pivotal missing link in providing medical services to all of these people. Many are being treated for symptoms to put out imminent fires while the root causes of their diseases are being undervalued and unaddressed, leaving chronic disease to smolder.

Our traditional western medicine model has evolved into treating symptoms with medications while failing to focus on the whole person and the underlying dysfunction that is the disease catalyst. This model is fueled by a fast-paced world, insurance companies, pharmaceutical companies, and the desire for a quick fix. Let me be clear, I am not insinuating that there are not amazing doctors across the country. It isn't the doctors that are failing us, it is the model. Our highly competent, highly skilled western medicine practitioners simply do not have more than 5-10 minutes on average during an appointment to address healthy living and lifestyle modifications. That is not enough.

My husband suffers from Ankylosing Spondylitis (AS). Ankylosing Spondylitis is an inflammatory arthritic disease that causes pain and stiffness. Over time, the inflammation can lead to bony fusions, making the spine rigid. The inflammation can also lead to a variety of other issues including inflammation of the eyes, costochondritis (chest pain that makes it difficult to breath), and heart disease. He spent almost 10 years, nearly reaching complete debility, without a diagnosis or treatment. He went on to spend the better part of a decade going from doctor to doctor, scan to scan, and was dismissed as maybe "crazy." This was occurring at the height of the Oxycontin/Opioid epidemic in the United States. During his time of searching for answers, he fell victim to being overlooked by legitimate doctors, as he was written off as a drug seeker with "invisible" pain. For the record, he never wanted, took, or was prescribed narcotics, nor did he ever ask his doctors for any narcotics. He is a pharmacist. If he had wanted pain pills, he would have gone to the "pill-mill" doctors, knowing very well where to find them. Doctors who were overly eager to prescribe narcotics were sadly plentiful at this time

Through networking and a bit of good fortune, he ended up at a primary care doctor's office, where he finally found someone to listen attentively. This doctor took the time to reflect on their training and consider his legitimate pain and debility to arrive at a presumed diagnosis. It was then that he was referred to a rheumatologist, where blood work and diagnostics, confirmed that he had been suffering from the chronic autoimmune disease that is Ankylosing Spondylitis. In other words, his body was attacking itself.

I didn't know my husband during his worst years with AS, while he was undiagnosed. When I met my husband, we were both working as pharmacists for a retail chain. He came to work at my store and explained to me how he had to sit down periodically during his shifts because of the pain. Some days were better than others, but it was clear the pain was frequent. I had just met the guy, and he gave me a disclaimer! He told me he had AS, and while I had briefly recalled learning about the disease in pharmacy school, I wasn't exactly familiar with it. As time went on and we went from being coworkers, to friends, then eventually started dating. I started to learn more about the disease and how it had affected not only the trajectory of his life, but the quality of his life. No disclaimer needed. We quickly fell in love despite his diagnosis.

My husband treats his AS with a Tumor Necrosis Factor (TNF) inhibitor. It is a drug he injects weekly that dampens his immune response to more or less "turn off" the autoimmune nature of the disease. The drug has been life changing for him. What was once debilitating pain turned into manageable daily pain. It was a step in the right direction from where he was without it. However, it is not without consequence. He gets every cold and virus that our kids bring home and gets it worse than the rest of us as a result. In addition, he is also subjected to a list of other risks associated with the drug.

My husband was diagnosed well over a decade ago and has since been living in constant pain with his dampened, but still present, symptoms.

This includes years of daily or weekly episodes of costochondritis (the feeling where he can't get a good breath), anxiety from the unknown, diffuse pain that travels through his body, immense fatigue, gastrointestinal issues, and the incidental cancellation of plans. The good news is, he can walk. He can work. The medication took away the debility he had previously suffered. For a while, he moved on from his diagnosis with a certain acceptance of the disease and gratitude for the medication that made it tolerable, as well as the physicians that found him answers.

Fast-forward, now in his 40s with two small kids and like many people, he added high cholesterol, high blood pressure, and increasing anxiety to the equation in addition to the AS diagnosis. More disease, more pills, less vigor, more fatigue, and no real solutions. As I thought back over my experience, I knew that inflammation was likely part of the real problem. This is when I started to wonder, "What can we do to quell his inflammatory state?"

I have been in the field of pharmacy for roughly 15 years now, dating back to my entry into the field as a pharmacy technician for the most fun place to shop (Bullseye, anyone?) I had an immediate passion for retail pharmacy as soon as I started. I came from the restaurant industry, and ironically, found a lot of parallels between bartending and retail pharmacy. Connecting with people across the counter, offering a listening ear, serving as a counselor, offering up a smile and warm energy to those that needed it, and of course, offering a product (drink or pill) to make someone feel a little better, these are the parts of my career that I loved.

I entered retail pharmacy with a passion to help people, but I wanted to help people on a deeper level than I was able to as a bartender. I wanted to make an impact on people's health journey when I entered pharmacy. While I can surely say that my career over the last 15 years has presented multiple opportunities to make an impact, I don't necessarily feel like I've been able to fully connect the dots and make a direct impact on people's health and lifestyle as a retail pharmacist.

We spend so much time training through school, rotations, internships, and in our personal quests for knowledge to build our clinician toolkit. I haven't had the time and space to use the tools in my toolkit in the ways that I've wanted. There have been many times I've wanted to help people more, but my job in retail pharmacy made it difficult. For example, while working at a retail chain, I saw a gentleman shopping for nutritional meal replacements for his diabetic wife. As a man devoted to caring for his wife, he just wanted to help her manage her diabetes. His lack of nutritional knowledge, while having been raised on meat and potatoes, coupled with his socioeconomic status, alluded to the fact that he was struggling to understand why his wife's blood sugar levels were not coming down. I asked him what kind of meals they were preparing, and he started with something along the lines of, "Well, I don't understand why her numbers aren't coming down. I've been cooking for her, and we aren't eating cakes, pies, and cookies anymore. I make pancakes for breakfast…"

Stop. Right. There. This guy needed a lot of help. He needed more help than I could provide in the 2 minutes I happened to have available. I helped as much as I could and pointed him in the right direction for the sugar-free protein drink for his wife. I gave the quickest explanation of why pancakes might not be the best breakfast option for his wife and got back to work. I felt defeated. I felt like I failed as a healthcare provider at that moment. Sadly, this is just one such example.

This is the problem with healthcare. I wanted to invite him to sit and chat. I wanted to go crazy and teach him all about carbohydrates. That wasn't possible, though. I was working in a busy retail pharmacy chain. They didn't pay me to sit with customers and help them. They surely didn't pay me to sit with customers and provide nutritional advice.

One day as I was scrolling on social media as I often do at the end of my day to unwind, I came across the Functional Medicine Pharmacist's Alliance Facebook group and joined shortly after it was created in 2018. I stayed dormant in the group for some time, giving thought to posts that piqued my interest, but never participated in the conversation. A chiropractor that I had seen during my pregnancy quit his practice and went into Functional Medicine, and that had really been the only other time in life that functional medicine was something I gave any thought to as a concept or practice. I joined the Facebook group because I like to network and honestly, I was curious about what those pharmacists were up to. I'm what we call in western Pennsylvania a "neb-nose," or someone who is always wanting to know what everyone is up to.

In full transparency, at the time I had a skewed, polarized view of functional medicine. I lumped it into the section of my brain that included questionable practices that may or may not actually work or have a valid place in medicine. Harsh, I know, so harsh. Please let me explain.

As a pharmacist, we are trained to critically evaluate scientific data. We are trained to look at different studies through different lenses, analyzing outcomes and challenging trial methods. We are trained to be data driven, critical thinkers who make decisions on the basis of scientific evidence and data. When I learned of functional medicine, I was under the impression that this field was NOT evidence based, but rather relied on a body of thought that included a lot of "maybes." I mean, have you seen the Wikipedia page on functional medicine?! Yikes. I didn't totally make that perspective up. I was, however, totally wrong.

As it turned out, that Functional Medicine Pharmacist's Alliance Facebook group opened my eyes to a whole new way of practicing as a healthcare provider. Over the months, I scrolled past evidence-based

A New Perspective Yields Hope for Change

information that was actually improving patient outcomes! I started thinking about the "pill for every ill" way of treating disease versus the "let's actually modulate the trigger for the disease to make it go away" approach.

Of course, everyone in the medical community wants to help our patients based on the latter approach, however, it's simply not how western medicine is generally executed. It's not how insurance companies reimburse providers, and it's not what patients expect. At large, our society and medical community are serving up the "pill for every ill" approach. We go to the doctor when we don't feel well and have the expectation that we will be given a prescription to make the symptoms go away.

All of this had me asking, "What if we didn't need to take a pill? What if we could just fix the problem in the first place? What if we help our bodies to heal themselves?" I now had a new perspective of functional medicine and an enormous amount of respect for the providers making real change in people's lives with it. I was excited that pharmacists were working to change the skewed perspective of functional medicine by delivering real, impactful, evidence-based solutions to chronic disease sufferers.

The thought crossed my mind that maybe this was the answer to the frustrations I had with my career. Maybe this was the space where I could fuel my passion for nutrition and healthy living. Maybe this is where I share my lifelong devotion to healthy living and change other people's lives. Maybe this can change my husband's life! I started thinking about my career more, too. I asked myself questions like, "Didn't I become a pharmacist to make a difference?", "Am I making a difference?" And then self-doubt crept in, and I began to think, "I don't know the first thing about functional medicine, so I can't do that!" The initial thoughts of "Maybe…?" were tabled.

Enter the year of the global pandemic, 2020. I was working in a hospital, and it became one big, long year of getting by. I was getting by in a lot of ways; with childcare, with sanity, by crazily washing groceries, trying to stay healthy, and so on. I am so thankful that my family all made it through, and my heart goes out to all of those that didn't get by, or even worse, didn't make it. All this to say, I didn't spend this time thinking about where I wanted to go next in my career. I spent it going to work and getting by. The entire year was one big stressful blur of work, sleep, stress, eat, and repeat for myself and my colleagues.

In the summer of 2021, with the pandemic seemingly quelled, I found myself fresh out of a professional leadership development program in which we were given a capstone project to devise a personal development plan. I loathed the project because I tend to avoid working on myself, however, this time it spurred a development plan that I didn't see coming. The project gave me a renewed hope for my profession that I needed. It propelled me to research how I could make room at the table for myself as a qualified and competent functional medicine practitioner. In true Gemini spirit, I'm always onto the next thing, headed in another direction, or planning something new. I was finishing the development program and discovered my next move through brainstorming for the capstone project. It was a push for something more. It was a push to pursue a passion. I was finally ready for the challenges ahead.

I penned my vision to pave my path towards my functional medicine career. I found a path where I could fuel my passion to help others to not just get well but, but more importantly, stay well through healthy living and getting to the root of their disease. I realized that I could turn my lifelong obsession with health and nutrition into something useful. I felt reinvigorated and ready to thrive. I felt inspired to help my husband find his way to better health and put out the fires burning inside his body. I felt hope.

With my excitement, I began further networking and made some connections that landed me in the hands of the dear Dr. Christine Manukyan. Dr. Christine is a pharmacist who broke out of the corporate world and into functional medicine. She is now paving the way for others, like myself, to learn how to do the same. I set up a connection call with her via Zoom and started to discuss the potential ways to break into functional medicine, as a pharmacist, and to learn how she might help as a business coach. Christine's energy is contagious. She is so easy to talk to and is one of those "instant friends" from the moment you meet her (even if it is virtually). The call was going great. It was a quiet Friday afternoon, my kids were at Grandma's, and my husband and I had gone for a morning bike ride. I felt energized and excited! Just as Dr. Christine and I were getting deeper into the conversation, my husband interrupted us. He had chest pain and I needed to get him to the ER. I abruptly ended the call.

What happens next isn't a heart attack story, or anything even exciting, really. I guess you could say the ride to the hospital was... thrilling? My husband begged me to pull over and call 911 as I sped down the highway, confident I would get him there faster than if we stopped to call an ambulance. Plus, I'm confident in my CPR skills, so there's that! He had minor chest pain that sent him into a panic attack but checked out fine at the ER. We left 3 hours later. Anticlimactic, I know! But here's the thing, it was a sign that I was right where I needed to be, and that I needed to help my husband. His body is in a perpetual state of inflammation with his autoimmune disease. His heart disease risk is exponentially worse than that of his peers with equally poor blood pressure and cholesterol. As a direct result, there is constant inflammation coursing through his body. We were still on edge, awaiting a stress test for peace of mind. I took this experience as a sign. The call with Christine, coupled with my husband's state of health, was enough. I decided my call to action had come, and it was time to get to work.

I was over the status quo. I was over my husband's inflammatory state. I was over my coworker's plight, going from doctor to doctor trying to get by with SIBO (small intestinal bacterial overgrowth), while on constant antibiotics and feeling unwell. I was over my mother-in-law not feeling well and suffering with fibromyalgia while she suffers through pain to care for my children. I was over the state of health that so many people close to me were in when there was an avenue to get to the root cause of these diseases. I realized that I could help these people I know and love to feel better. I know I am going to make an enormous impact on the quality of life for the people that I love, and people that I haven't yet met, but will love.

So, here I am. A pharmacist. Entering the world of functional medicine, where I have the opportunity to show the world that pharmacists can make an impact in this arena and in the functional medicine space. I am in awe of some of the ladies in that Facebook group that I mentioned earlier. They are thought leaders who took a chance and paved the way for pharmacists in functional medicine. We have the training and background to get to the breakthroughs that can change the lives of those who we have the opportunity to serve. And there is even evidence to practice by. Did you catch that? Real evidence, people!

I am currently in the early stages of launching my practice, *Planted to Thrive*™. It is going to be a labor of love, rooted in my training and life experiences that have brought me to this point. I will work with my clients to get to the root cause of their disease to help them find their way to wellness. I am going to share my passion for health and wellness with the world in a whole new way, and I cannot wait!

I have joined the *Pharm to Table* team of pharmacists to provide functional medicine services in a collaborative environment to further foster my clinical skills development and provide optimized outcomes for my clients. I have started clinical training with Functional Medicine University and will be a Certified Functional Medicine Practitioner by early 2022. This extra clinical knowledge is icing on the cake to the thorough training of pharmacy school.

I'm no stranger to "starting over." As I said earlier, pharmacy is not my first career, and I will always love all you people in the restaurant industry! Remember that husband I talked about? Well, he happens to be the third man I've called "husband" (no judgement zone, right?!) Starting over, for me, has involved a lot of heartache and hard work. Entering functional medicine feels more like a "reinvention" to me, rather than "starting over." I'm not leaving pharmacy, but I'm reinventing the way I practice it, and I couldn't be more excited. Pharmacists are creating a space in functional medicine to transform the way we deliver healthcare, and I'm extremely honored to be a part of it. Please stay tuned as I prepare to share *Planted to Thrive*™ with the world. I am thrilled to be embarking on this journey of entrepreneurship while partaking in the revolution that pharmacists are bringing to the Functional Medicine space.

If I could give advice to myself as I navigated many of my "starting over" challenges in life, it would be to always follow your passion. To love yourself first and nurture your gifts so that you can share them with the world. Don't chase a title and don't chase a checklist of things that you are "supposed" to do. Life has no timeline, so don't make decisions like there is. Enjoy your journey and listen to your heart. Share your passion with the world, and believe that you are worthy, because you are. Don't think about what you want to do, put what you want to do into action. Believe in yourself! And never allow self-limiting beliefs to hold you back from your true potential. Never stop dreaming, and never stop learning. Live your life asking yourself these questions: When I'm gone, what will I have left behind? When I'm gone, where will my impact remain?

ABOUT DR. BROOKE SPINO

Dr. Brooke Spino is a functional medicine practitioner, pharmacist, and founder and CEO of *Planted to Thrive*™. She believes in plant heavy nutrition and our bodies amazing capacity to heal. She empowers her clients to achieve optimal health by uncovering and correcting the catalysts of disease. Brooke has passionately worked in community pharmacy for 15 years, collaborating with providers and patients in order to optimize medication regimens and health outcomes with healthy living strategies and an aim to decrease pill burden.

Dr. Brooke is a devoted wife, mom, and stepmom who loves family bike rides, yoga, veggies, dancing, and CBD. She received her Doctor of Pharmacy degree from the Lake Erie College of Osteopathic Medicine and is a Diplomat of the Pharmacy Leadership Academy through the American Society of Health System Pharmacists. Dr. Brooke is a Cannabis Health Professional in the state of Pennsylvania. She will receive the designation of Certified Functional Medicine Practitioner from Functional Medicine University in 2021 and is continuing her studies with the Institute for Functional Medicine.

In her practice, she is on a mission to educate her clients on targeted nutrition, stress management, CBD, and overall wellness strategies so that they can transform their gut health, inflammatory state, and overall well-being. Her vision is to help shift the health and mindset of her clients so that they can stop living to "get by" and start truly thriving.

www.plantedtothrive.com | drbrookespino@plantedtothrive.com | IG: @planted_to_thrive

Chapter 7

THERE IS A BETTER WAY!

By Emily Saparito, PharmD

"Of all of the things she did to follow her dreams, believing in herself was the most important one."
– Spirit Daughter

Do you remember when you were a child, and everyone brought their lunches and snacks to school in little lunchboxes? Do you remember the kids who always had the "good" snacks and those who had the "boring" snacks? And by "good," I mean junk food. And by "boring," I mean healthy. Well, I was that kid bringing granola and baby carrots to school every day. Even my bread had seeds in it! I can thank my dear mother for that today, but not at the time, of course. At that time, I wanted Doritos and Dunkaroos in my lunchbox!

Fast-forward to my college days, and my mother struck again. She read *Clean* by Dr. Alejandro Junger, and decided to do this cleanse, but needed an accountability partner. I agreed to do it with her since she promised that all I would have to do is show up to drink the already prepared smoothies and eat the organic quinoa and chicken. I thought, "Count me in, can't get any easier than that!" It was not one of those starvation cleanses you hear about celebrities doing on the news. I was never hungry. It was, at the most basic level, a whole food cleanse. Just eat whole foods! No dairy, no processed foods, no junk, essentially. After three weeks, I shed some weight and fought off some excess bloat. The results I experienced included increased energy, brighter skin and eyes, improved digestion, and better sleep, just to name a few. And those were just the things I noticed from the outside! My insides were most likely thanking me tenfold. That was my first introduction to the power of lifestyle change and food as medicine. That power is severely underestimated, unfortunately to the detriment of most western cultures. Ironically, that is where my background originates, the power of the pill. Without my extensive Pharmacy Doctorate background, though, I would not understand the full potential of functional medicine. I would not understand the anatomy and physiology of the human body or the pharmacology of nutritional supplementation. Combining the two worlds of conventional medicine and functional medicine, sets me apart from others, and allows me to get to the root cause of suffering in a safe and effective manner.

After graduating and getting licensed, I went to work as a retail pharmacist with various leadership positions. During this time, I became a wife and mother of three, my proudest accomplishment to date. With three kids under four years of age, let's face it, you have to be young for this! After my first child was born, I hit a wall. I felt stuck and felt like there was no way for me to do what I really wanted to do, which was be a stay-at-home mom. I know it sounds crazy after all the hard work I put into becoming a pharmacist, but it's just how I felt. I couldn't help it. I also thought pharmacy school was going to be the hardest thing I ever did, but boy was I in for a surprise after having kids! Nothing compared to the pure joy I felt when I was at home with my daughter. That lasted about a year, until basically I became numb to the anger and sadness from going back to work in the corporate world. I did not heal that wound and I accepted my dreary fate of missing bedtimes, missing events, and missing precious moments. My family could painstakingly tell you about the infinite number of times I called or texted them throughout the days, constantly making sure my daughter didn't walk yet. I did not want to miss her first steps. I felt like it would've burned a hole through my soul, and I do not say that lightly. Thankfully, as far as I know, I was there to witness her first steps. Let me be clear though, I did not hate my job, I actually loved my job. I went into pharmacy because I'm a nerd and organic chemistry excites me. It was a way I could use that education to help people when they needed it most. I love being that person! Pharmacists are the most approachable and knowledgeable healthcare workers in any capacity, which is something I'm proud of.

In those days, I did a lot of research on what the best books for anger were. I bought on, but I never read it. It was already shameful enough that I had bought it. I had to suppress the anger. Which are what women, especially moms, are expected to do. I keep it on my desk as a reminder of how far I've come. I realize now that you can't serve other people, if you can't serve yourself. There are a lot of issues with that statement when you're a mother, though. Historically, that's what moms are expected to do. We're expected to serve others, even if that means emptying their own tank. Historically, moms don't ask for, or heaven forbid, accept help. Still today, moms are praised and glorified for "doing it all" and having it all together, all the time. The more they accomplish by themselves, the better. How exhausting! But when is enough, enough? Mom guilt is something I struggle with, and am still working on, but progress is progress. Whether it's pressure from outside sources, or unnecessary pressure put on myself, the first step was realizing that the anger is there, and then putting in the work to unlearn it.

After this realization of discovering I'm not stuck, I started having books like *Untamed* by Glennon Doyle, on my desk. Motherhood forced me to realize that, in fact, one person *cannot* do it all. My husband always says, "there is growth in vulnerability." Who would think that accepting help, or accepting failure, could put one in such a vulnerable position? I will tell you exactly who, moms! But who would benefit most from seeing that vulnerability? Children! Think of the strength they will see, when mom chooses herself when she needs to, chooses to help, and sometimes falls, but gets back up. That is the type of mom I want my children to see. Not one who lets life happen to them instead of opening up and chasing the life they want. I have realized so many life-changing things since becoming a mother. There is always more to learn, and always growth to be had, but most importantly, there is always a better way.

After that brief and slightly dark introduction, I assume you, the reader, can tell how obsessed with my children I am. When I became pregnant with my first child, I became overly conscious about what I was putting *on* my body and not so much about what was going into my body, because hey, I was pregnant! When it came to the baby after she was born, however, I was neurotic about what I was putting in and on both of our bodies. The skin is, after all, like a big mouth, absorbing anything it comes in contact with. Only the best for the baby, though. Gotta start them young! Their bodies are too precious, innocent, and angelic for this world. I always knew about the dangers of cleaning products and perfumes, for example, but I didn't start taking them that seriously, until I became pregnant. I would buy all natural products when it was convenient, and I tried the new cleaning trends when I heard of them, but I was not in it for the long hall. The fact that these toxic products are everywhere makes it seem as if they're safe, when in reality, they can cause things like allergies, cancer, developmental concerns in children, reproductive issues, liver damage, and neurotoxicity, just to name a few. This includes in our food, (hello pesticides, herbicides, and fungicides!) It was shocking to find out that some of the ingredients in my shampoo and perfume were hormone disruptors. My first thought was that pregnancy is very dependent on hormones, so I will eliminate those toxins as much as realistically possible, starting as soon as possible. My second thought was, "How could these companies and my country's laws even allow these to be sold to any consumer, much less a pregnant one?" Worse than that, the "green screening" most companies do, where they put a picture of a pet with some leaves, and label it as "all-natural" when that's just not the truth. They are not natural at all. To the naked eye, and to the uninformed consumer, it actually makes you feel like you're buying something safe. There is nobody governing these statements, unfortunately. From that point on, I knew that if I wanted to protect myself, I would have to do my own research to arm myself with real knowledge. As a mom, I'm always questioning if what I'm doing is right. Now, I was on high alert!

In my daughter's first 3-6 months after birth, she suffered from a mild case of eczema. Of course, to me, that was catastrophic. Again, as a mom, I'm asking myself, "What did I do wrong? What could I have done better?" I poured myself into any research I could find on eczema, and the first thing available to me was from the conventional medicine standpoint. Conventional medicine doesn't even mention a cause or a cure! And yes, if you're following the premise of this story, I'm sure you could guess her pediatrician said, "Don't worry, it's normal she'll grow out of it." To me, that sounds like a nice way of covering up the fact that you don't know and you're not willing to put in the work to find out why. So, the only thing available to me were treatment options. Steroids, to be specific. With my pharmacist background, I knew the repercussions and side effects of those treatments, especially steroids. The most common being steroid withdrawal syndrome, in which the chronic use of topical steroids for more than 2 weeks can result in the original rash coming back with a vengeance. It can also cause thinning of the skin when babies already have thin skin to begin with. Babies also already have increased systemic absorption and easily absorb anything put on their skin. After all, eczema treatment options are addressing the symptoms, not the true cause. I'd like to point out that I am not steroid mongering. I fully understand the need for them, in the right situations and conditions. I was not about to go down that route with my daughter right away, without trying anything else first, though. My heart was telling me to listen to my inner voice, and that there must be a better way to help her. There must be a root cause, and there must be a reason for her suffering. I would follow the signs and do whatever it took to figure it out. That is the power of functional medicine. It's tailored to the individual, and we solve the puzzle, no matter how complicated it is.

I started looking more alternatively and holistically. What I found was distressing, yet also, not surprising. What is eczema? It is a symptom or sign from the body that something is out of balance. Dermatologic issues, specifically, are a sign that the body is in toxic overload. The liver, kidneys, and gut have roles in detoxifying the body. Functional medicine teaches that everybody's body is different, therefore has different toxicity tolerances, and different ways of responding to it. Toxicities range from environmental, like chemicals pollutants, allergens, heavy metals (specifically copper for eczema), molds, bacteria, viruses, and alike. It could simply be exposure to something that the individual's body can't handle, such as food. Toxicities in today's world are, unfortunately, ubiquitous. When the liver, kidneys, and/or gut, cannot keep up with the toxicities, they get pushed out of the skin causing the red, itchy, scaly, rough, inflamed, irritated effect. Eczema is not only caused by gut dysfunction and detoxifying issues, but also hormone dysfunction and stress.

You might be asking yourself, "Can a baby be stressed?" Yes! Imagine crying for so long because your back just itches, and your dear mother thinks you're hungry and keeps trying to shove a bottle in your mouth instead? Before you get scared of this toxicity and dysfunction talk, let me tell you, I was actually relieved! I now had a starting point! The only place I could go from here was up.

What is unproductive to treating this condition? Overloading the body with more toxins! As Maya Angelou wisely states, "When we know better, we do better." So, what is the first step in healing from eczema? Diet and lifestyle change! I was still exclusively nursing my daughter, so I cut out as many toxins and commonly known eczema triggers from my life as realistically possible. This included diet restrictions as well, which was quite possibly the hardest part of it all. After trial and error with many "clean" and eczema prone formulation skin care lines, I found a skincare line from France, that was specially formulated to treat eczema. Europe has far more strict guidelines, as far as ingredients in topical products go, as compared to the U.S. Specifically, there are over 1,300 chemicals banned for use in cosmetics in Europe, and only 11 in the US.

My daughter's eczema did clear up after a few months, and all was well. I felt like a weight was lifted off of my shoulders. I realize now that a few months is the minimum length of time it takes to identify a root cause and begin the healing process. The stress of it took a serious toll on myself and my husband, though. We thought to ourselves, "We can't be the only parents looking for solid answers," but I knew I was one of very few parents who have the medical background to be able to piece together the puzzle. This sparked my passion to help other families going through the same thing. It's one thing to be told as an adult, by a physician, that what you're experiencing is "normal," and not to worry about it, but it's another thing for children to be told that. Years go by until someone finally listens to you, because you've gotten to the point of desperation. To me, though, "normal" is *not* necessarily healthy. And when it comes to our children's health, we do worry. And we don't have years and years to waste while they're suffering, when they don't have to be. This holistic approach identifies the root cause. It takes time and commitment, and boy, is it worth it! You either spend time suffering or you spend time giving your body what it needs to heal. Either way, you're spending time. As easy as popping a pill might be, if you're not eating nutritionally balanced whole foods, not moving your body, and not getting quality sleep, there is no pill that can help you. There is a better way.

At this point, I had been incorporating functional medicine in my own life for about 10 years, although I didn't recognize it as that. It was official, I had turned into my (modern day) mother. Ordering salads while at restaurants, bringing grapes to the park, eating gluten-free bread, and drinking almond milk. My kids were doing the same! I had one advantage though, they didn't know Doritos or Dunkaroos existed, yet. The plan, of course, is to keep it that way as long as possible, but also not deprive them. When they're teenagers, they'll have their fair share of ice cream and donuts, I'm sure. All kidding aside, preventative care was key in my life. Again, "When we know better, we do better." And I am so grateful for the knowledge my medical background provides me, in order to achieve real wellness for my family and me.

Did I learn about the importance of improving nutrition and gut health in pharmacy school? Or that gut inflammatory markers in children and adults are different? Of course not! But understanding the gut allowed me to further learn how to improve wellness, within the whole body, and tailor it to the individual. My understanding of conventional medicine allowed me to connect the dots of the body systems and uncover the true cause of suffering.

Despite not learning about all of this in school, I am grateful for all the knowledge I have gained and am ready to share it with other families and their children. 11% of children suffer from eczema. Eczema patients are twice as likely to have depression or anxiety, as compared to those who don't. Who can blame them? Eczema is commonly seen in patients and families with asthma and other allergies. Ultimately, that is what I am trying to prevent; the progression of eczema to allergies and asthma, which is otherwise known as the "atopic triad." As many people know, allergies and asthma can be life-threatening. If given the chance to possibly prevent concurrent diseases that are life-threatening, wouldn't you take it, too?

Motherhood and this path to wellness has inspired me to branch out from my traditional role as a pharmacist, to a new role of entrepreneurship, doing something I love. More than anything in the world, I want to be home with my children and not miss a single thing (until they're teenagers who are too cool for me, of course. Will they even know what the word "cool" means?) Before I became a mother, I did not know I was going to feel that way. The thought never even crossed my mind. I thought I would return to work, just like any other mom I'd seen, or like the way the movies portray it. I don't know why it's such a secret that mothers long to be home with their children, or why it's so taboo to talk about it. Maybe because it's too painful to talk about. After discovering my love for functional medicine and realizing that I could truly help people heal without medications, I felt like I discovered my calling.

Entrepreneurship could allow me to be home more and be the mother I always wanted to be, while using my medical and holistic background to turn people's lives around. There was only one thing standing in my way, me! I had never done anything like this before, could I do it? During the time I spent thinking about it, trying to find some reason why or why not to go for it, I went on a hike with my daughter. What my mother and I thought was a beginner level hike, turned out to be more expert level. Of course, my mother was the one who invited us. We did not know what we were getting into when we said, "Yes!" At the scariest point of the hike, the steepest, sharpest, most slippery point, I held onto my daughter for dear life. I even carried her for some of it. At her age, she did not sense the intensity of it. We did not stop until we got to the top. I was finally able to breathe, and I said, "Woah! We didn't know it was going to be like this, but we just kept going and look, we did it!" After I said that, I thought, "Were those words meant for my daughter and this hike? Or were they for myself and my life's decisions right now?" It was my sign to keep going all-in, even if I don't know what it's going to be like in the end. I called Dr. Christine Manukyan soon after that and told her I was all-in! The road that led me to cross paths with Dr. Christine was not paved by accident, by myself, or even by her. Going on that 1000ft incline hike with my mom was not an accident, it was purpose-filled, even though I didn't know where it was leading me at the time. The road that led me to that trail and to cross paths with Dr. Christine was a divine encounter, intended to happen, at that time, for a reason. I believe that you are reading this book at this time, for a distinct reason. Are you ready to say, "Yes!" and step into the life you're called to live?

ABOUT DR. EMILY SAPARITO

Dr. Emily Saparito is a Certified Functional Medicine Specialist™ from Functional Medicine Business Academy™ and Holistic Health Coach. She is a proud wife and mother of three wonderful children. Dr. Saparito is the CEO and founder of an online Functional Medicine Practice, *Health Empowerment and Radiant Transformation LLC*, (HEART). In this fully virtual practice, she helps overwhelmed parents navigate their child's diagnosis of eczema, allergies, and asthma, without medications, through her unique and holistic Better Way Program.

Dr. Saparito has spent 8 years as a community pharmacist, where she was first introduced to the far-reaching capacity of eczema, allergy, and asthma suffering. After experiencing her own encounter with childhood eczema with her first child, she made the decision to trust her inner voice and try a root cause approach before diving into the underworld of medications for her precious baby. This led her to the discovery that protocols like improving gut health and detoxing are, in fact, possible! Yes, even for babies! After her proven success, she felt called to help other parents stuck in the same place who are stuck without the proper support they need and are unaware of the natural solutions available.

Dr. Saparito is on a mission to set parents free. Free from the chains of their child's unnecessary suffering, and free them from using potentially harmful medications used to treat the presenting symptoms, rather than the root cause of the problem. Using the functional medicine approach, she is able to help parents and children find healing from the inside out. *There Is a Better Way.*

www.dremilysaparito.com | dr.emilysaparito@gmail.com | IG: @dr. emilysaparito

Chapter 8

FAILURE IS NOT A TRAIT, BUT RATHER, A TEMPORARY EVENT

By Gaby Udabor, FNP-C

"When you know better, you do better."
– Maya Angelou

In the years since I discovered functional medicine, the quote above, by Maya Angelou, has become my mantra. Yes, now I know better about finding functional medicine and now I can confidently declare my health is better in mind, body and spirit. How amazing my life has changed in the last three years discovering functional medicine which I would also call progressive medicine.

Well, let's go back to 2018 in the years before I found functional medicine. I remember one particular day in 2018 like it was yesterday. I decided that I had enough and was desperate to find something else. That girl was tired physically and mentally and, at the time, I decided that I needed to find an alternative way of medicine, one that didn't depend entirely on traditional medicine. It was my 3rd time getting positive results on the H. pylori test and I remember the moment when I saw the lab result, I broke into tears. *H. pylori* (Helicobacter pylori) is a type of bacteria. These germs can enter your body and live in your digestive tract. After many years, they can cause sores, called ulcers, in the lining of your stomach or the upper part of your small intestine. For some people, an infection can lead to stomach cancer.

The tears of frustration were from multiple lab panels, multiple doctor visits, and all different types of medications, mostly antibiotics. It was so painful going through all of this and to still see my health declining. My gut had been torn apart from all the medications! Depression started creeping in, on and off weight loss, fatigue and it just felt like too many issues for me to deal with. To summarize, I was not feeling well! It was even more frustrating as I am someone who could be considered "the health gut girl." That, along with being a nurse practitioner, I just felt so defeated that I could not help myself. There were so many questions I asked myself in these times such as, "Would I have to deal with all these multiple GI problems, specifically, the H. pylori infection and chronic constipation for the rest of my life? Why are so many patients on so many prescription meds and don't seem to be getting better?"

There should be a better way, I thought. Although I was trained in the traditional/conventional medical model, where we are taught to wait for a disease and then treat it. I have always been interested in preventive medicine and was never a big fan of just prescribing medications to my patient. I always liked to teach my patients. Even with my limited time in the clinics, I could teach about basic nutrition and lifestyle from the little I know. As you probably know, the nutrition and lifestyle thing are not taught much in the nurse practitioner program as well as in other medical professions such as medical doctors and physician assistants.

In my desperate need to find other alternatives, I found functional medicine. I remembered some months ago, I had been following this functional medicine provider on Facebook and was always intrigued by the before and after pictures of her clients, and all the testimonials of healing from functional medicine. I saved some of her posts, so I could go back to those posts, and go through them again. I kind of started "stalking" this functional medicine provider's Facebook page and checking in on her website. I continued to do this for some weeks before I finally felt convinced that this was the way to go. I really needed help and I believed this provider could help me.

I went ahead and contacted her to set up an appointment for an introductory call. It was a short call in which I summarized my issues, and with all confidence, she assured me that she could help. I was delighted and went ahead to schedule the first 90 minutes comprehensive case review. You see, when she told me about this case review, I was already feeling so much hope because this is something I had never done before in my struggles with my illness. So, there I was, on the day of my first official consultation with her where she went through all my labs and lifestyle from A-Z. She asked about my diet and my stress level before showing me all the patterns in my labs indicating a trend that I had more things than just H. pylori that need to be addressed.

Lo and behold, by the end of this 90-minute consultation, I was a full-on believer in the functional medicine model. I jokingly told my functional medicine practitioner that I would like to be like her when I grew up and asked how I could do that. All the knowledge and connecting of all the dots with my health was just so impressive, and I wondered why this was not taught in my nurse practitioner program? I needed this change because I did not want to go down the same path of my parents, grandparents, uncles and aunties. I want to set this pace for my kids, so they do not go through what I have gone through. I need this change to help my family, my husband, my parents, my brothers, and whoever out there cares to listen and implement healthy patterns. Even if they do just 10% of what I recommend with functional medicine, they would see a change in their lives. After my consultation, I went ahead to do some more labs, and based on what my practitioner put together, she suspected that I may have an autoimmune disease, specifically associated with my thyroid.

To give you some more context, for many years the only thyroid labs that had been checked for were TSH (thyroid stimulating hormone) and t4, which always showed as "normal." With that, my doctors just let me be. So, I was told that I was doing ok, but deep within me, I knew something was still wrong. With me working with my functional medicine practitioner, however, she recommended that I do a full thyroid panel, which showed everything that may be wrong with my thyroid. To be truthful, this aspect hit me hard, and I wondered why I never thought of this, especially being a nurse practitioner. Also, why in the world did my health care providers never think of testing these things? The signs were there, abdominal pain, chronic constipation, fatigue, on and off weight loss, and so much more. Well, my full thyroid panel test results came and lo and behold, it showed my thyroid antibodies were elevated. It was then that they confirmed I had Hashimoto's, which is an autoimmune disease of the thyroid.

As time went on, I realized that the resistance of the H. pylori treatments was a blessing in disguise. This is because, if I had "healed" from the antibiotic treatments all those years, I would never have sought out functional medicine, and probably would have now been overcome with other diseases, like the autoimmune disease that none of my health care providers ever addressed. I would not have been able to discover that my son had some allergies that were causing him to be asthmatic. I would have never realized how powerful food is to heal the body. The list goes on and on.

During those times before I found the functional medicine practitioner, I was also in a season of my life where I was questioning if being a nurse practitioner was the right profession for me. I had discussed with my husband that I was thinking about maybe changing to a registered dietician/nutritionist, as I have so much love for nutrition, and it looked like I could help more people that way. I was also frustrated with the health care model that was ruled by insurance, not to mention the number of patients in which I only had a limited amount of time to see them. I was just not feeling that I was giving my best and was not fulfilling the reasons I became a nurse practitioner in the first place. The inspiration to further pursue functional medicine was found in the transformation of my gut heath within 6 months of treatment. I was dealing with these issues for a decade! Say what?! It was a no-brainer for me to continue down this path. It gave me hope that I could still be a great nurse practitioner while incorporating these functional medicine principles. I did not necessarily have to change my profession, but I could combine the best of both worlds — conventional medicine and functional medicine. I found out that my education in Western medicine/conventional medicine made me a better functional medicine practitioner because I could clearly see the gaps in Western medicine, being that I had practiced that for many years. I could then take what I learned from that education and apply the functional medicine principles to fill it up or, better yet not allow those gaps to even be there. It is just amazing.

I am now in the phase of my life where I just want to shout it out from the mountain top to whoever is ready to listen to me, "functional medicine is the key to wellness!" I feel so empowered that I feel I could tackle anything that wants to jeopardize my health, my family, and/or my clients. Towards the end of 2019, I decided that I wanted to have my own virtual practice offering functional medicine and integrative health services, as I believe this will give me the best opportunity to help as many women as possible with their health issues. I was able to complete Level 1 in the School of Applied Functional Medicine (SAFM), which allows me to see the changes in my own health even more! This further boosted my confidence and hope in the healthcare world. In addition to getting my education in functional medicine, I also decided to work with a business functional medicine coach. The investment was steep, but it gave me much needed structure, hope, and confidence that I could build this practice. Of course, there are obstacles in the way, but I will keep going to see where this will lead.

My goals in building this practice are that, as a mother of 4 who is very family oriented, I will have flexibility, financial freedom, and also the opportunity to reach out to help people from all over the world. It was freeing to not be bound to the fact that they may not be able to heal. I believe I have accomplished a lot since finding functional medicine. I have now incorporated my knowledge about functional medicine into my passions, cooking, and further education. I have been able to start a YouTube channel which offers different resources. Also, on my Facebook and Instagram, you will find me talking about different wellness topics, often. I share my knowledge on how women could get their health back, holistically. My gratitude for finding functional medicine is overwhelming. These are just some of the ways I hope to continue building my functional medicine and integrative practice for women.

As a woman of color, and the fact there are not a lot of functional medicine providers out there, this journey can be extremely challenging. This leads me to long to be a great example, and hopefully, encourage people like me, to see the possibility to become strong healthcare providers. We need diversity among providers to help maximize the amount of people we can help with their health, both as the patient/client, and also as a healthy healthcare provider. I believe progressive medicine needs to incorporate a functional medicine model into all facets of healthcare education. This includes programs for nurses, nurse practitioners, physician assistants, medical doctors, pharmacists, and nutritionists. I believe that incorporating even just 50% of the functional medicine model in all practices, will go a long way towards helping individuals, clients, and patients in their healing journey

CALL TO ACTION: "Don't give up the fight. Failure is not a trait, but rather, a temporary event." I came up with this mantra from my life experiences and base it on where my hopes and dreams keep going. What I'd like to expand on from here is that whatever you are going through in your life, keep on pushing through until you are able to see a change. It may take years, but I firmly believe that where there is life, there is hope. The things I have learned as a mother of four, a health care provider, an entrepreneur, and just living life in general, is that we are going to fail (or fall) a lot. There will be many times you feel inadequate, have imposter syndrome, are comparing yourself to others, and in general just feel like a total failure. What you need to remember is that failure is not a *trait* but rather *an event* that it is not meant to stay, instead, you can overcome it. And how do you overcome it? You get up, dust yourself off and keep going. This is what I keep doing. I would not say it has been an easy road as I transitioned into this way of functional medicine after working for many years in the conventional/traditional medicine model.

I know some of you who are in the health field, be it nurse practitioners, pharmacists, MDS, physician assistants, or nutritionists, might be reading this book and may have already been thinking about other forms of medicine that could be out there. It could also be that you are not even a healthcare professional, but just an individual who is interested in improving your health or has been dealing with a chronic illness. Maybe you're just tired of getting tired, you want to feel better. It might be that you are frustrated with the conventional medicine model and do not know what to do about it. Or maybe you are wanting to make a change but are afraid of the judgment from your colleagues, your family, your friends. I say this because I also have experienced many of these questions and fears. There have been times that I have been viewed like I'm selling snake oil. Some will say functional medicine is pseudoscience. Well for me, I have personally experienced a great amount of change in my life, and through my clients' lives, since finding functional medicine and strongly believe in it. I would not be writing this chapter otherwise. I have experienced, firsthand, the powerful healing associated with this type of medicine. I still believe in conventional medicine, so don't get me wrong, because I know it still serves a purpose. I personally will continue to use it for my clients, patients, as well as for myself when it's appropriate and necessary. For those of you who are a health care provider in any way, or have been trained using the conventional medicine model, know that you are actually at a greater advantage. Use that information to be an exceptionally great healthcare provider, by combining the two worlds and filling in the gaps.

There are a couple of things I wish I had known before beginning this adventure, and I am excited to share them with you to help you step into rewriting your story:

1. Find a group of like-minded people. If you are a healthcare professional, look for a group of professionals by searching for your similar interests and/or credentials, and if you cannot find one, you can find a non-health professional group with similar interests. There are many of them on Facebook, so it really isn't hard to find a like-

minded community to plug into. To make it easy, look up, "functional medicine," "holistic health," or "integrative medicine." Any of these groups could be helpful to begin learning about this progressive way of medicine. And as a bonus, it gives you a supportive community. Like I mentioned earlier, it can be challenging when you add this type of medicine to your life, as it is still not well known by many people when compared to conventional medicine. This means it's even more important to find groups like this to give you encouragement and motivation that you might not get from your colleagues, family members, or friends. You can also look for professionals that are already practicing functional medicine and follow them on social media. They always have great sources of information. Feel free to follow me @gabyuhealthhub to find my health talks, cooking tips, and so much more.

2. If you are a healthcare professional wanting to start your own functional medicine practice, I highly recommend hiring a business coach. A business coach who is also knowledgeable in functional/integrative medicine can help you grow faster and stronger, pulling from their own expertise and experience. You might want to go through mini interviews with a few different types of coaches to see how they fit with your personality, as one person's coach might not be the right fit for you. There has to be an alignment. Fortunately, a lot of the business coaches do offer free consultation calls before you fully commit to working with them. Take advantage of those. This process will also apply to you if you are seeking someone to help with your personal, your health issues/goals. You can go through this process of having those free consultation calls to see who a good fit would be. Once you find your coach, you will be able to jump all in.

It is by no accident that you are reading this book. Just opening it, and reading through the stories, is already streamlining the process of stepping into this world of functional medicine. If you reach out to any of us women who are sharing our stories in this book, one of us can surely help you to reach your health goals and even to help you start your own practice. What are you waiting for? Stop overthinking it and go for it! I'll promise you this- you will be glad you did. You are on your way to achieve that balance in mind, body, and spirit. If I can do it, I know you can too. I will leave you with Maya Angelou's quote that I talked about in the very beginning, "when you know better, you do better." You *can* do better.

ABOUT GABY UDABOR

Gaby Udabor is a functional medicine health consultant, Woman Wellness Strategist, Family Nurse Practitioner, speaker, best-selling author, Gaby U Show podcast host, and a mother of 4. She is the co-owner and founder of Gaby U Health & Wellness Hub, a 100% online functional medicine and integrative practice for women. She helps women to reclaim and optimize their health by balancing their hormones, lose stubborn weight, restore gut health, and improve overall mood. For over 17 years, Gaby Udabor has worked in a wide range of different health care settings from primary care clinics, nursing homes, and weight loss clinics.

Gaby Udabor's has been featured on the STORRIE™ Podcast, Carpe Diem Living, Rock Movers, When doctors say, "we don't know", Nurse Strong, Nurses Outside the Box, Women Living Healthy & On Purpose. She has also been a speaker in the Dominators annual conference. Gaby is also found on YouTube, Instagram, and various other places where she is educating or speaking to others about preventive health and healthy cooking.

Gaby's approach and passion for functional medicine began because of her personal battle with on and off fatigue and gut health issues that lasted for almost a decade. After many visits to multiple providers, labs, prescription medications, and still not getting better, she decided things needed to change.

Gaby's mission is to help women, who share similar health issues, heal from the inside out. She is determined to empower women not to give up and to know that there is still hope to reclaim and a way to optimize their health. Gaby takes the time to put together a personalized plan for each of her clients, learn their uniqueness from their personal health history, and dig deep into what has or has not worked in the past. At the end of this intake process, every client is presented with an individualized plan, and this is where the true healing becomes possible.

www.gabyuhealthhub.com | office@gabyuhealthhub | IG: @gabyuhealthhub

Chapter 9

THE POWER OF SELF-HEALING COMES FROM WITHIN

By Hona Kandi, ND, MBA

"We sacrifice our health in order to make wealth, then we sacrifice our wealth in order to get back our health."
– Dalai Lama.

Moving to the United States from our native country, due to religious beliefs, was not an easy decision made by my parents. I was not confident with their decision and was nervous about the school setting in a country and culture that I was unfamiliar with. We settled into Virginia, where I began attending a local high school. I was hopeful for a better life but was still very worried about how to start a new life. Looking back, I am happy, now, that I could dream about my future in real life and not daydream anymore. Working full time and going to school full-time might have been a little difficult, but I motivated myself to have enough energy and hope every day in order to financially provide for my family. I had a dream, and I was going to do anything possible to accomplish it.

When I started college, I was thrilled, but clueless. It felt amazing that I could continue my education, but I did not know how to make it through my first semester. However, what I knew was that failure is a path to success. Even if I fail, I have learned how to progress in life from my own experiences. That is the path to create any accomplishment. I knew that the main difference between a person who is not successful and a person who is, is not because of the lack of knowledge and strength; it is because of the lack of willpower. I started to build a growth mindset to change my perspective because I believed I was capable of growth that can lead me to achieve success. I also know everyone is born with natural abilities and intellect that influence a person's achievements in life. Therefore, I told myself that I should grab this great opportunity and not let it pass me by. I looked for support from every resource I could get from college, and surprisingly I made it through smoothly for all these years.

Unquestionably, I believe many people in this world are in the same situation as me. Having gone through a hard time to survive, I would say it is fortune and hope that brings me to this new stage in life. In the beginning, it was challenging for me to declare my major because the world I grew up in is so different from where I am now. However, I always knew in my heart that I love to help others and relieve their pain. Therefore, I started my undergrad in biology to obtain knowledge in science. After completing my biology degree, I went on to obtain an MBA to help me tie my experience with business and science together.

I learned people could get relief without conventional care, and I became passionate about functional medicine and nutrition. After assessing my passions and abilities, I decided to work in a nutritional environment and further grow my knowledge in nutrition, natural health, and wellness. I am faithful and certain that I can restore health for those who are seeking optimal health. I further researched the details of what I could do and where I could get started. Additionally, my interest in helping others began when I talked to and worked with other healthcare providers about the satisfaction they get from helping people and relieving their pains. I am here now to help my community and help them with improving their lifestyle.

First, I must acknowledge that my own personal belief system is constantly changing and is never stationary. The more I learn, the more I grow. I find that I often must alter my past belief structure. That is why I am here on this planet to learn and to grow. At the very core of my belief system, we are body, mind, and soul. These three entities are united and connected. When one is in a state of conflict, the other parts are equally affected, whether we are mindful of it or not. Our feelings and emotions have a great impact on our physical health; our spiritual connection has an enormous impact on the other two entities. Therefore, to heal our physical bodies, it may, at times, be necessary to address underlying emotions, thoughts, and internal conflict as well.

My second belief is that through nature, on this planet, we have everything we need to not only survive but to thrive. Most medicines we need to heal are provided to us mostly in nature- the air we breathe, the water we drink, the sun we get exposed to daily are all available to us in nature. With the help of nature, our bodies are endowed with an innate power to regrow and heal themselves. All that is required is to give the proper nutrients to work with and remove the impeding materials, and the body will do the rest! We need to be empowered and recognize that health and healing comes from within.

My third valuable learning experience is that the short and long-term quality of life is determined by choice rather than by chance, and sickness is a choice. When health problems are identified before they become serious, people can make changes that positively impact their health for a lifetime. We all know that no one willingly chooses sickness over health. So, we need to ask ourselves, "What does our body require? What is the wellness plan to keep us away from any disease state?" However, we need to think about if we want to stay healthy. For example, when health problems are identified before they become serious, people can make changes that positively impact their long-term health. Reaching optimal health is a product of how we eat, drink, think and do. Health is a choice and is a matter of balance. The cells in our body are seeking a healthy balance to thrive. Our physical body, mind, and spirit require proper food for nutrients, air for oxygen, water for hydration, sunshine, exercise, sleep, and love. Not providing an adequate amount of these will result in disease, and it is upon many factors such as mental and physical weakness, stresses, and toxic exposures. When our body is healthy, it is more resilient and can more effectively recover and heal. We choose what we put in our mouth every day, and we decide to exercise or meditate daily or not. What we choose every day has a great impact on our health. This is not to denigrate, but to empower individuals, because we have the ability to *choose* health. We have the power to give our body what it requires doing what it's designed to do, which is to heal itself.

Today, more than ever, there is a necessity for nutritional supplementation. I wish this was not true, but unfortunately, the food that our ancestors had access to is not available to us anymore. This can be blamed on factory farming, the spread of GMOs, and the distribution of chemicals and processed food. Even if we consume 100% organic and plant-based foods all the time, our soil is depleted in nutrients, not just in this country but also worldwide. Now, adding GMOs and spraying all conventional crops with pesticides and herbicides further reduces the nutritional value of our food. Additionally, we consume a diet high in GMOs, chemicals, sugar, additives, and preservatives; the cells in our body get less resistant and accumulate toxins. This will create a dramatic effect on our overall health for the worse. Therefore, it is necessary to consult with a health care provider with a nutrition background and functional medicine practice to get us on a good nutritional supplementation regimen.

Both the soil and minerals don't have balanced pH and are deficient in minerals, so the food supply is not as nutritious as it used to be. The excess acid load is a result of dietary choices and poor stress responses. If our soul and body are connected, we must make the absolute best choices by following nature and nurture for a healthy life. For example, we need to make sure we eat food from balanced pH soil, as well as non-GMO and organic foods, to prevent a state of acidosis, depletion of bone tissue, and chronic conditions. That being said, we cannot only live and rely on supplements alone. A balanced diet is the best source of essential vitamins and minerals. Vitamins and minerals are involved in cell signaling, growth, repair and energy production. Food should be our primary source of nutrition. Therefore, it is vital to know that consuming various foods promotes health and prevents chronic conditions that may lead to obesity, anxiety, and cardiovascular issues. If we don't eat a nutritious variety of foods, taking supplements alone might help us get some nutrients. However, it is vital to know that supplements can't take the place of a variety of nutritious foods, which are very important to creating a healthy diet. The main principle of reaching a good amount of nutrition comes from consuming high-quality, fresh, and whole foods; therefore, it is important to remember to reach for foods grown organically or biodynamically. The focus should be on eating plant-based foods that include fresh vegetables, fruits, grains, beans, fermented foods, and toasted nuts and seeds. These foods hold an active enzyme that improves the digestive system.

To increase the benefits of eating healthy, it is better to avoid ingesting the same foods repeatedly because it increases the possibility of becoming sensitive to those foods, especially if the digestion system is weak or compromised. Choosing the rainbow, or a variety of foods, can limit the problem. To enhance eating habits, the relationship with food needs to be acknowledged as most populations might not have the proper knowledge about nutrition, and upon food shopping, they may struggle to choose what is good or bad food. Therefore, our eating plan should be rich in complex carbohydrates chosen from vegetables, whole grains and legumes (lentils, beans, peas). High-quality protein may include pasture raised/organic eggs, deep, cold-water fish such as salmon, and sardines. More protein sources can come from nuts and seeds. It is essential to eat healthy fats and focus on healthy omega-3 essential fats that enhance energy production. Let health care providers know what the best plan for you is, and they might choose a different plan based on your health condition. Today, there is a growing need to find a health and wellness and a functional medicine practitioner with knowledge of nutrition, can provide the needed tools to develop healthy relationships with foods.

Furthermore, we live, undeniably, in a toxic world. Today, there is not a single person in this world who is not exposed to hundreds of toxic substances daily. Our cells in our bodies are overrun every day that is beyond our grasp and awareness. The radioactive particles in the air, EMF pollution, heavy metals, BPA, plastic, chemicals in our personal hygiene carry hundreds of different chemicals people apply on their bodies. There are toxic chemicals in the clothes we wear, and the laundry detergents we use, the pesticides and herbicides sprayed in our fruit and vegetables, and in the hormones and antibiotics used in factory farms. How does the body function at all when it is overburdened with these toxins? Being exposed to so many chemicals, we need to do the right thing to improve our optimal health. So, detoxification should play a big part in our community, and is important for everyone to understand. It supports the body we have the better and maintains vitality. Cleansing has a significant impact on well-being. It gets rid of the damage left by the burden of this toxic load and frees up cellular energy that we need to apply to our lifestyle changes. When toxins accumulate, it can change our metabolism, causing us to become more tired, sluggish, and less efficient. There are many ways that this could occur, such as hydrotherapy, clay baths, salt and soda baths, skin brushing exercises to promote sweating, far-infrared sauna therapy, chelation therapy, DMSA, EDTA, and many more.

I also learned that the mind and body have a powerful bond. Thoughts and emotions can directly affect all the organs in the body. Feelings can positively affect the mind and body. On the other hand, unhealthy thoughts add to the burdens and cause chronic conditions. Movement and engaging in enjoyable, aerobic activities are crucial for cognitive and skeletal development in children and the elderly. Exercise encourages healthy aging. Techniques such as meditation, abdominal breathing, and salt and soda baths are basic and simple methods to implement at home to improve the quality of life. Physical activity enables the body to repair deficits, while a lack of physical activity leads to heart problems and bone health issues. Sustainable exercise should be enjoyable and moderate, rather than extreme activities that feel burdensome. Because the mind and body are connected, collaborative movement is vital for the physical and spiritual mind. The best activities need to be combined with abdominal breathing and physical activities. Jogging and walking can be effective physical activities for bone health. Specifically, walking for 45 minutes daily in a beautiful, peaceful, and quiet place is preferable. Walking and jogging help to improve circulation and oxygen levels, which helps bone health. Deep breathing while walking speeds up lymph flow. Physical activity helps with mindfulness and activates the body's healing functions.

I was always fascinated by science from a very young age. The peak of my interest in the world of nutrition, health, and wellness was primarily motivated by my own son, who developed skin rashes at 6 months old. His pediatrician diagnosed his skin issues as eczema, and he was prescribed antibiotics and cortisone. She also assured me that his eczema condition could last until he was 2 years old. I decided to take matters into my own hands and searched for some alternative treatments, and I happened to discover a test for delayed food and chemical sensitivities. Since he was under 2 and his immune system was very close to mine, I tested. As soon as the results were ready, I consulted one of the clinical specialists on staff and applied my results to my son. I followed their program, and we chose immune system-friendly foods that helped with enhancing metabolism. We also added the right nutritional supplementation regimen for him, according to his results. His eczema, diagnosed by his medical doctor, was almost gone after 2 weeks. After 2 months, we were able to clear his skin, and no further skin issues appeared on his face or body. I was so thankful for the outcome and that he did not need to be on medication at such a young age. Finding out the burden on his immune system, and enhancing it, was the answer to my son's skin concern. I pinpointed my son's problems with nutrition as the root cause of his health and skin challenges. In the end, we were able to reverse all his symptoms without any use of medication. After identifying the problems, the focus was on solutions for better health.

Furthermore, I also watched as my mom faced some unwanted pains and developed sleep issues. She started experiencing some complex situations that were not curable. It took her a full year with conventional medicine, and still there was no progress to her pains. I asked her to apply the functional medicine approach, as well as see a practitioner who can spend time with her and listen to her story and look into her problems. They were able to look at the interactions among her genetics with the environmental and lifestyle factors to support the unique expression of health and vitality for her. Moving more towards an alternative care and functional medicine approach, her condition significantly improved. If you need to know what functional medicine is, it is a biology and physiology-based approach that focuses on the root cause of health conditions. A functional medicine provider takes time to listen to the client's full life history, which allows the health professional to better understand the reason(s) why the client has reached their current state of health. It uses the model that ensures clients get results where other conventional and complementary therapists fail. And for my mom, the functional medicine plan was to pinpoint exactly what things she needed to avoid and what nutritional supplements to add to her daily regimen. Doing that helped her identify a customized, anti-inflammatory diet. Removing the bad stuff, such as environmental toxins and adding good stuff within a diet that she could easily digest and assimilate, made it possible for her to manage and even reverse her conditions. It was straightforward for her, she just had to implement the findings into her lifestyle. She was pleased and excited to have real answers to her care concerns. The pain is almost gone, and her sleep has improved for the better.

This was valuable learning that made me decide to explore my lifelong passion for health & wellness. I became a firm believer that sickness is a choice rather than a chance. Healing the body with what it can digest, assimilate, and eliminate what it can't and choose long-lasting lifestyle changes can all help us regain our health and feel better than ever. Our body is very powerful and self-healing, and we only need to give it the right nutrition to let it thrive. Although life, in general, is one continuous learning experience, I have learned a lot from my own personal experiences. We are constantly seeking optimal health. I have learned that quality of life is determined by choice rather than chance; it is a matter of what we eat and drink and what we think and do. Nutrients to our body are like the fuel for the engines. We all must take responsibility for our life, our choices, and our own health care. It is important to ensure that our modern diet and lifestyle choices promote our overall health. We need to stay mindful and balanced while following these basic foundations, including drinking water, getting a good amount of sleep, exercising, and eating nutritious, whole food to support optimal health and allow for more movement and freedom daily. Following these basic foundations will allow us to live healthier lives and be more present as we age. Following approaches that enhance the body's innate ability to prevent sickness, repair, and restore health should be at the heart of our wellness journey.

Goals help us grow and give us wisdom and purpose in life. Success promotes happiness, and happiness in return promotes greater health. We can set goals that guide us and provide a sense of direction, self-excitement, and self-worth. Nutrition is a path to health and an important factor in living. My goal in life is to educate myself and others in ways that restore and maintain a healthy balance in the body's internal environment that will prevent further illness and help family and friends achieve their health goals. I am interested in personalized wellness programs that are designed to empower me as an individual to live a full and healthy life. I have a passion for health and well-being, and I love making things work efficiently, starting with the body we live in. It is my goal to live in the flow of life, free of physical ailments, emotional heaviness, stress, doubt, and anxiety by giving my family the gift of true healing, self-love, and freedom leading to unlimited happiness. These are the philosophies and beliefs I hold on to, which will guide me in my long-term wellness.

ABOUT DR. HONA KANDI

Dr. Hona Kandi is a board-certified Naturopath and functional health coach. She is passionate about changing lives by optimizing the health and wellness of those she works with individually. Hona believes that health care should not be viewed as a one-size-fits-all plan, instead, it needs to be personalized to fit the person.

Before becoming a functional health consultant, she started her undergrad in biology to obtain science knowledge while working at traditional healthcare organizations. After completing her biology degree, she received an MBA to help her tie her experience with business and science together. While completing her MBA, she started working for a nutraceutical company, where she was able to work with functional medicine and integrative Health care practitioners. She learned people could get relief without conventional care, and she became passionate about functional medicine and nutrition. Hona has continued expanding her education in health and wellness and became a certified natural health practitioner. With over seven years of experience working in integrative health settings, Hona is now in a master's program working to obtain her nutrition degree in order to become a clinical nutritionist.

Dr. Hona is passionate about coaching and educating, and she is now a frequent speaker at functional health practitioner coaching groups. Her goal is to provide the best practice for individuals who need assistance by discovering and addressing the root cause of symptoms and the body's internal imbalances. She believes everyone deserves to be healthy and feel their best. She is passionate about optimizing health and will use the best tool at her disposal to provide effective approaches for optimal health. This is the most gratifying work for her, as she often witnesses true health transformations in her private practice. She views the body as one integrative web with a balance between different organ systems. Her approach is to consider all aspects of one's health history, including food, stress, environmental toxicity, hormone imbalances, and looks at the body as a whole. We all deserve to live a symptom-free life.

healthconsulting.kandi@gmail.com | IG: @honakandi

Chapter 10

MNDSHFT FOR ELEVATED HEALTH, AN ALIGNED CAREER, AND A VIBRANT LIFE

By Jennifer Wheeler, MS, MSN, FMP, NP-C

> *"The formula for a life of health and vitality is quite simple: Spend energy on that which aligns, choose with intention and create ownership with discipline."*
>
> – Jennifer Wheeler

The overhead announcement was loud and clear, "Code blue tennis court... Code blue tennis court." The moment had arrived. The moment I knew *may* happen at some point in my fitness management career, but to be honest, I never thought it actually would. I was trained in CPR, yes, but would I actually know what to do if that moment ever occurred? I was about to find out. I dropped the weights I was using for my personal training client and started running. Thoughts started flooding my mind like, "Is it a heart attack? Will they be breathing? What is the updated compression to breath ratio?" I arrived at the scene, assessed the situation, assigned roles, and began compressions. At that point, I could not feel a pulse. Somewhere in one of the main heart vessels, the blood was blocked from continuing down its path to provide life-sustaining oxygen. I wasn't thinking about any of this, though. I only thought of what needed to be done at that moment. Right then, the AED arrived. This is the man-made machine that attempts to shock a heart back into rhythm. Pads were placed, I called out to "all stand clear" and shock! Analyzing rhythm, all stand clear, and shock again. Then we waited, for what felt like an hour. Finally, a heart rhythm was detected. Oh my gosh, it worked! The heart was beating, the life was saved.

Never would I have imagined the emotional highs and lows of experiencing that situation. We saved a life and saved a family from the grief of a lost life. If we were not there, that life would have ended. I was shaking, but beyond thankful and knew, at that moment, that I was exactly where I was meant to be. Could this experience have saved my life as well? Somehow my journey through studying music, theology, adolescent psychology, and exercise science (I know, what a combo!) brought me to this pivotal moment. I knew I was meant for more and was capable of more. As I always have, I followed my gut instinct and decided to return to university to further my studies once again, this time in the medical field. It was time to help people *live*.

My studies and career in nursing were largely spent at one main university, where I entered into the field of Neurosurgical Intensive Care, directly after my nursing program. I looked back on that simple, but powerful moment providing life-saving CPR, and couldn't believe I was now keeping patients alive with multiple medication drips and leveling tubes to balance the cerebrospinal fluid in their brain. It was intense and I was challenged, but I loved it. I always believed in furthering my education, and the concept of being a life-long learner was just innate. I thought about what was next and knew the "level-up" for me was to become a Nurse Anesthetist.

After early admittance, I was all set to begin my program. Just then, my husband and I found out we were expecting our first child, who is now our oldest daughter. Wait a minute, I'm following my gut, my destiny, my path, but I wasn't able to begin this program due to the time commitment it required. I was excited for our family to grow but was now confused as to where I was headed professionally.

Have you ever wondered if you were on the "right path?" Afraid that the choices you are making are not in alignment with who you are or what you were born to accomplish? I always struggled with those questions, often wondering if what I was doing was actually what I was meant to be doing. After all, I had so many passions in life. I started out studying piano, then theology and psychology, then pursued a masters in physiology, and then nursing. I also love to run, dance, play piano, sing and swim. Does this thought pattern sound familiar? I thought I was alone, but came to find out, many colleagues and friends in this field were conflicted with similar thoughts. How was it I couldn't just decide what to do in life? It took a while, and many pivots, for me to embrace that this was who I was as a person. I am a multi-passionate individual who will learn and grow in many areas of life, and that is ok! In fact, it is a beautiful thing that allows me to truly live my life to the fullest. I wasn't going to be the person who decided to be a veterinarian at age 9 and stuck with it their whole life. Once I allowed that pressure to fall away, I began to step into my own path, the one that is aligned with who I am in all of my passions, experiences, and loves for this beautiful life. I am able to assess how I feel about an opportunity or a choice and change my path forward. I allow my energy to be my guide.

Having my daughter at the same time I was supposed to start anesthesia school, allowed me to explore other possibilities in my career, and slowed me down enough to remember the foundation on which I have always wanted to build my life upon. Living a life feeling healthy, vibrant and well was always my priority. I had always been active through dancing, running, snowboarding, triathlons, field hockey, and being outdoors, and as I grew older, I also learned about the benefits of nourishment, nutrition, and eating foods straight from the earth. Interpreting this as a meaningful direction, I completed my second master's degree, this time in nursing, and began practicing as a primary care nurse practitioner. Beautiful ending, right? Not quite. Isn't a primary care provider supposed to help you live a long and healthy life? How was this possible if I didn't have the time or resources to actually address the root causes of a disease or absence of vitality? I quickly realized that 10-minute visits with patients to address symptoms, a pharmaceutical approach to treatment, and a focus on managing disease, was not what the majority of my patients needed or even wanted. Health is not the absence of disease; health is living a life of vitality. In traditional medicine, the standard labs are compared to a broad range of labs and are not a real indication of optimal functioning. My patients were not experiencing a healthy life, and to be honest, neither was I!

I felt stuck. Stuck not being able to help my patients, exhausted and burnt out from years of studying, having 2 children (I commonly see nutrient deficiencies after multiple births causing major symptoms in my daily practice), growing my career and family simultaneously, without clarity on what my body actually needed to feel at its best. How did I just complete a high-level master's degree and see patients every day as a nurse practitioner, but still not understand how to truly address my patients' health needs? Not only did I need more time with my patients, but I also needed more time for myself, and needed more focus and direction to align my own health. After multiple doctors and specialists' visits, I still couldn't figure out why I was exhausted with symptoms of nausea, dizziness, insomnia, headaches, constipation and so many other chronic symptoms. How was I, a primary care NP with endless resources, unable to find real answers? I read and researched, exercised, and took the latest vitamin, protein, collagen supplements that I would hear about, and yet, still did not feel healthy and vibrant. I now know these were just a shot in the dark and a waste of money, but at the time, I hoped to feel better. I remained frustrated and stuck, and still knew I was not reaching my maximum potential.

This led me to make some major changes in my career and my life. The first step was to embrace the mindset shift: I not only can feel better -- but I can also heal and thrive. The thing is, you don't have to stay where you are if you don't believe in it. Just because you were taught something or are doing what the world has said is "right", doesn't mean you don't have the ability to disrupt the mold and choose that which aligns, that which elevates, that which ignites. Make the choice. Take the first step. I fully believed there was a better solution, and I was determined to find it. The body is meticulously and beautifully designed. Being a woman who is passionate about physiology, nutrition, and function, it was time to explore human design at a new, deeper level, so I could help others and myself, to truly live. And not just to live, but to actually live well.

This pursuit led me to the discovery of functional medicine through research, of course (are you getting to know me yet?) I grew to passionately believe in it and see the changes it offers through my own experience. Through advanced, in-depth testing, the deepest dive into my health history, and an exploration of my personal health goals, the functional medicine approach has allowed me to discover what choices I needed to make in order to support my bio-individuality (what my body actually needs to function well.) This was it. How beautiful is the feeling of alignment? I was extremely clear that functional medicine is my destined path. All of the intricately woven experiences that led me to study so many areas of health, medicine, and wellness, were coming together for this next chapter of my life!

You may be reading this and wondering, "What exactly is functional medicine?" The functional medicine model is an individualized, science-based approach, that empowers you and your practitioner to work together to address the underlying causes of disease and promote optimal wellness. It doesn't aim to diagnose a particular disease and, in turn, prescribe a medication that is aimed to "treat" that disease and the symptoms associated with it. Instead, it requires a detailed understanding of each client's genetic, biochemical, and lifestyle factors. Once the necessary information is collected, it leverages that data to direct personalized solutions that lead to improved health outcomes. In shifting the disease-centered focus of traditional medical practices to a biochemical individuality approach, functional medicine addresses the whole person, not just an isolated set of symptoms.

It was through functional medicine that I learned how the multiple rounds of antibiotics I received for infections throughout my childhood, had played a major role in creating an imbalance in my gut, a.k.a. dysbiosis. I also was able to understand the negative effects of the dietary choices I made throughout high school and college and their long-reaching snowball effect towards elevated toxic load and hormone imbalance. How is it that in medical school we spend little to no time on the concept of micronutrients and the absolute necessity for vitamins, mineral, and nutrient levels necessary in order to be optimal for our cells to actually function? Here we are, in the traditional model, diagnosing major disease processes and searching for the best medication combo to merely keep those symptoms at bay. This model is forgetting the very simple concept that our cells need a beautiful balance of nutrients to work properly, otherwise cell changes (aka disease), will occur. The comprehensive functional medicine approach included an exploration into how I felt about my childhood, my adolescence, and major life transitions, from an emotional standpoint. I learned that at any given moment, one's life experiences can completely change the trajectory of one's health outcomes.

It didn't take long to make the decision to transform the way I practice medicine. There was no holding me back. I knew that there was so much more to offer my clientele, true needle-movers, towards creating a life of vibrant health. I had a heart-to-heart with my husband, who luckily, along with my family, has been one of my biggest cheerleaders. This revelation brought us both to open a wellness collective together in a local town, as a space for like-minded practitioners to make a collective impact on individual and community wellness. My husband and I sat on the Chicago River while visiting the city, to see one of my favorite music legends, Van Morrison, and there we brainstormed the launch of my private practice, *MNDSHFT Health*™. We talked about the pros and cons, ins and outs, and most importantly, he asked me *why*? And so, I shared my whole story, an in-depth view at what I was struggling with internally, both in my own health and in what I was able to provide for my patients. When you ask yourself WHY, you are then opening the path to creating alignment in your decisions. When we are clear on what is important to us, the decision-making process becomes so easy: is it aligned with who I am? Or is it not aligned?

I actually first started out with a different practice and company name. This begins to speak to the many changes and pivots I have made as an entrepreneur in the wellness space, in order to adapt and grow as both a business owner and a practitioner. We had a full rebrand, and this occurred less than a year into practice. My entrepreneurial journey rapidly expanded due to a commitment to research, learning, trial and error. This is not the path for an individual who wants to repeat the same processes day in and day out. This is for the driven person who is ok with change, ready to research and respond, and is committed to ongoing learning in the entrepreneurial space. It continues to hold true as *MNDSHFT* enters its new phase of expansion with the onboarding of 3 new expert functional medicine practitioners and it's second cognitive wellness strategist who focuses solely on mindset strategy and cognition for our high-level clientele. As we continue to refine, our focus remains steady: provide a concierge-level experience that revolutionizes the health of high-performance individuals.

MNDSHFT Health™ is the premier virtual functional medicine practice for health optimization and longevity. I created a practice that has very strong differentiating factors that are key when establishing yourself in a field with many practitioners that are offering similar services. Our main differentiating factors include high-level clinical support from the top functional medicine clinicians, effective and clear direction on what is happening in the body, why it's happening and how to restore and refine one's health, access and convenience with the tested structure of our MNDSHFT Method, and a focus on protecting the time and energy of our clientele with simple, sustainable solutions. The practice has grown exponentially since inception, all with the mindset of pivoting with the climate of business. It *is not* about the vast number of years you have studied and elaborate information you want to teach your clientele, it *is* about what your niche clientele needs to learn and implement in order to move the needle and light a fire on their health journey (with the other stuff sprinkled in as needed).

The reason I chose the name *MNDSHFT* is because it takes a massive shift in mindset to reclaim life-changing wellness and performance for yourself. When you choose to view health as your greatest asset, and not an afterthought or obligation, you open the doors to living a life of vitality. There is a beauty to making choices that are aligned with who you are, and what you are meant to accomplish. It opens the doors to further growth and abundance. Time spent studying functional medicine, and working intimately with clients, has allowed our offerings and services to continue to grow and be refined. In creating the *MNDSHFT Method*, we now have a proven framework that other practitioners on our team can learn and implement. Yes, of course our recommendations and protocols are still individualized, but the approach in which we address common themes, has a structure and focus allowing for clear execution and sustainable results. An exclusive part of the *MNDSHFT Method* focuses on defining and refining ones' optimal health choices. These daily practices have the power to support or sabotage our mental and physical health. The *MNDSHFT Method* allows our clients to set the foundation for optimal cell function and minimal toxic burden, which are two of our main goals in order to achieve a healthy body and a vibrant life.

The choice to practice this way has not only changed my professional life but continues to enrich our family life as well. Clarity allows for meaningful decision-making. Decision-making leads to impact and growth. As for our bodies, if we are not clear on the unique physiological needs of our body, how are we able to make the best choices towards achieving optimal health? The same goes for our business. If we are not clear on our *why*, decision-making will be haphazard, and will leave us feeling stuck. If we remain stuck and struggling, we are not moving forward, and we are not growing. Clarity and discipline are the keys to growth.

My goal for myself, for my family, for my practice, and for my clients is still very simple. My goal is to *live*. As my company continues to grow,

I remain committed to life-long learning. We learn intrinsically as a growing team of wellness strategists. We learn extrinsically through clinical research, as well as experience with our clientele, and understanding what they truly need in order to elevate and align their health. I believe it is possible, as a practitioner, to design a model that fits your unique passions. This is beautifully coupled with what your tribe is looking for as well! It all starts with the common theme of this story, knowing who you are and not being afraid to take the next step when you feel that stirring feeling from within. I'm on a mission to refine wellness and change the tide of women's health potential. I am passionately committed to lighting a spark, so that each person can claim strength and freedom in the knowledge of understanding their unique body. I am confident this will create the vitality and longevity so many long for, although everything is a personal choice. It is through the power of clarity and choice, that we have the opportunity and the gift, to truly live.

ABOUT JENNIFER WHEELER

Nurse Practitioner, Jennifer Wheeler, is revolutionizing the health of high performing women. She is a driven healthcare professional who is providing clear and sustainable solutions, in order to help others, live with intention, experience vitality, and create alignment in work and life, with vibrant health as the end-goal. Jennifer specializes in elevating energy, mood, nutrition, sleep, gut health, optimal cell function & minimal toxic burden.

With 20+ years in the healthcare landscape, Jennifer chose to disrupt the traditional model and provide true solutions for optimal wellness. During the time she practiced as a board-certified primary care nurse practitioner, she found the traditional medical model to lack focus and clarity on the root cause of a patient's symptoms. Very little time is traditionally spent on the true needle-movers for optimal aging and vibrant well-being, and Jennifer is on a journey to change this.

Jennifer is the CEO, founder, and expert functional medicine practitioner of her company, *MNDSHFT Health2. MNDSHFT Health*™ is a first of its kind, high-level, Health Mastermind, based on advanced functional medicine principles, personalized protocols, mindset transformation, and the unique biochemical needs of each woman's body & mind. Jennifer has developed The MNDSHFT Method™ which is a simplicity meets strategy approach to mindset, nutrition, gut health and stress.

Jennifer is on a mission to change the tide of women's health potential. She is committed to lighting the way for women to claim strength and freedom in the knowledge of understanding their unique body and how to create vitality & longevity through personal lifestyle choices.

www.mndshfthealth.com | jennifer@mndshfthealth.com | IG: @mndshfthealth

Chapter 11

BEGINNING MY JOURNEY WITH FUNCTIONAL MEDICINE

By Kristina Telhami,
Doctor of Pharmacy Candidate (PharmD), 2022

"If we wait until we're ready, we'll be waiting for the rest of our lives."
– Lemony Snicket

Ever since I was a little girl, I always made sure everything was perfect. I had the perfect schedule, even in kindergarten. I got home from school, quickly headed over to my desk, and finished all of my homework right away. I never waited to do anything last minute, and I was always efficient with my time, even from a young age. I have always had this drive to be ahead of the game and never wanted to procrastinate on anything. Working hard has always been important to me, and I never wanted my work to be anything less than amazing. Since the beginning, organization and determination have been a part of my life and continue to be a foundational part of who I am.

My parents always supported me in everything I did throughout my childhood. There was never a time when they told me I couldn't do something, and I am so thankful to have parents like them in my life. One example of this is when I went from playing soccer, to doing gymnastics, to lacrosse, then to rugby. I went to various summer camps, and even begged my parents to take me to a horse-back riding camp, even though it was very expensive. They never told me no, and instead always encouraged me to do the things I am passionate about. My parents were born in the Middle East, where there were not a lot of opportunities like there are here. Because they grew up with almost nothing, they made sure they gave their children the best they could. Whether that was home cooked meals, taking us to the best private schools, sports, or traveling around the world at a young age, they did it all for us. The love they have for my siblings and I, in large part, is the reason that I am where I am today. Without them, I wouldn't be graduating from pharmacy school and writing my own chapter in a book, at the age of 26.

In middle school, I transferred from a small private school, in a class of 8 students, to a public school, with almost 1,000 students in Oakland, California. I transferred in the middle of the school year and knew absolutely no one at my new school. What I did not realize at the time was that middle school would be one of the worst experiences of my life. Being the "new girl," I was bullied, and people talked about me behind my back, constantly. One girl, specifically, disliked me so much that she emailed the students at my previous school about how horrible I was, and continually made fun of me. As if that wasn't enough, this girl then went on to share those emails to the entire school and call me both fat and ugly. I could have never predicted how much those two words would linger, and affect me, for far too many years.

Both science and math have always been a passion and a strong suit of mine. So much so that in school, I even won second place in our 6th grade Matheletes competition. I fell in love with Chemistry, ever since taking it in the 8th grade, and knew that one day I would be doing something in the science field. Because of this passion, I went to San Diego State University for undergraduate school and got my Bachelor of Science in Chemistry with an emphasis in Biochemistry. I remember wondering exactly what I would do with a chemistry degree, but I knew there were endless possibilities for me.

College was not easy for me, however. I struggled a lot with both my mental and physical health. I joined a sorority in hopes of finding my best friends for life or just finding a close group of friends, which can be hard at such a large university. Rather than making a lot of friends, I felt like I had none. I have never felt so alone, even while being in a sorority with over 300 girls. I constantly cried myself to sleep, felt like no one wanted to be my friend, and truly wanted to leave college and go home. I always thought something was wrong with me, and I continuously criticized all aspects of myself. It felt like no one liked me, and the other girls in my sorority always made me feel like I was never good enough to be their friend. This led to a downward spiral of negative self-talk and constantly trying to change my personality, so others would like me. I never felt like I could be myself, and I was constantly trying to fit into a different group of friends throughout each year of college. Even doing so, I still felt alone.

Attending San Diego State University, I had never felt so ugly or self-conscious. The people there were so beautiful, and I looked at myself in the mirror and criticized everything about myself. I hated the way I looked, I hated how fat my legs were, I hated my lower stomach fat, and I hated my arms. I kept thinking back to that girl in middle school and how she would tell me how ugly and fat I was. Eventually, I took all of this anger and hatred for myself and put it to the gym. I ran at least 7 miles and spent 2 hours at the gym every single day. I wanted to look thin, in hopes that people would actually like me if I looked thinner. This mindset quickly caused a downward spiral in my health. Not only was my physical health declining, but so was my mental health. The only thing I could think about throughout the entire day was exercising and "healthy" eating. I would not allow myself to eat more than 1200 calories a day and if I did go over this amount, I made sure I ran an extra 3 miles the next day to compensate. This cycle continued throughout my entire college experience, and as may be expected, I was not in a good headspace.

During this time, I was underweight, not sleeping well, and was having constant anxiety or panic attacks, even in class. My grades began declining towards the end of my third year simply because I could not focus on my class. I felt like I had no energy, and my brain was not functioning optimally. The truth is, I was not fueling my body properly, which made me constantly feel weak. Even getting to my lowest weight, I still looked in the mirror and thought I was overweight, not pretty enough, and continued to fight against my body. To this day, I still wonder how I was making it through the day and passing my exams while running 7 miles every morning, with not one day off of exercise and not eating enough food.

Something a lot of people do not know about me is that I had Amenorrhea for 8 years. Amenorrhea is a term used to describe the absence of a period. You read that right. Eight years without a real period. Back in high school, I remember having a regular period for a year and then, all of a sudden, it disappeared out of nowhere. Naturally, my mom took me to the doctor who took one look at me and told me to lose weight in my stomach area in order to get my period back. She then recommended I get on birth control. I was not overweight in high school, but I was a little inflamed and could have definitely been exercising more and eating better. At the age of 14, my doctor told me I should go on a diet, eat little to no carbohydrates, and then start the pill. I truly thought this was what I should be doing, because what else was I supposed to do? Listening to my doctor was all I knew to do at the time.

It is important to note that being on hormonal birth control and menstruating because of the pill is not the same as a natural period. Birth control is feeding your body synthetic hormones and masks your body's natural hormonal production. Contrary to popular belief, taking hormonal birth control is damaging your body's hormones and health rather than benefiting it. As for me, because I was taking it for so long, my body was not able to naturally produce the hormones I needed. Looking back, I cannot believe my doctor told me that in order to have a period, I needed to be on birth control! Rather than looking at the underlying cause of my missing period, my doctor had me take a simple pill to give me a monthly cycle.

What I did not realize at the time, was that the personal care products I was using on a daily basis were also causing me to have hormonal imbalances. As it turns out, a lot of skincare, cleaning, and personal care products contain chemicals, also known as "endocrine disruptors" which interfere with our body's hormones and are linked to a variety of health issues. I learned that your skin is your largest organ, and anything you put on it will absorb directly into your systemic circulation. Finding this out led me to change all of my products to non-toxic, which drastically improved my hormonal balance and overall health. The majority of the products I was using were disrupting my natural hormonal production and caused even more hormonal issues. So, why wasn't the doctor telling me this information? Why didn't they ask me about my lifestyle, diet, or products I was using? This was the beginning of my journey to discovering functional medicine.

On top of hormonal issues, my digestive health was something I struggled with in the past. In 2010, I went to a gastrointestinal doctor with stomach pain, knowing that I had a lot of digestive issues. They immediately put me on a PPI, also known as a "proton-pump-inhibitor."

A PPI drastically lowers your stomach acid, which you need in order to digest and absorb your food. What I did not know at the time, was that using this long-term can actually cause more harm than benefit. The doctors used this to treat my stomach issues, and again, failed to get to the root cause of my pain. Not once did they ask me what I was eating or how I managed my stress levels. I had no idea that the food I was eating, my lifestyle, and my stress levels were all contributing to my gut issues. Not only that, but your gut microbiome plays a huge role in your overall digestive health, immune system, hormones, and even your metabolism and mood. In our digestive tract, we have both good and bad bacteria. We need a good gut flora in order to maintain our health, and an imbalance of the beneficial flora can cause harm to our health. This is why focusing on our gut health, by eating real whole foods and taking care of our body, causes positive results for our overall health.

My digestive health throughout college was also suffering, especially during the spring of 2017. There was a period of time when I had chronic diarrhea for 2 months during my last semester of college. During this time, I quickly went to the doctor, where they told me to take Imodium, a commonly used anti-diarrheal drug, and I was advised to drink some Gatorade. After a week of this not working, I went back to my gastrointestinal doctor, where they decided to take a stool sample. This stool sample was only testing for H. pylori and parasites, but they did not do a complete and in-depth stool analysis panel that could test for more root causes. I was frustrated when everything came back as "normal" and all I was told was it could be related to my stress and that it should go away with time. The following 6 months I continued to have issues and I knew I had to do something. I started researching the root causes of gut issues and found a holistic health coach and functional medicine nutritionist who specializes in gut issues. I started seeing these practitioners, and they ran a full stool panel, where it showed not only what bad bacteria and yeast may be growing, but also showed what good bacteria I already had in my gut. This type of stool test shows an in-depth summary of what imbalances you have and whether you're digesting your food correctly, as well as what organs may be damaged. Through this panel, I found out I had a Candida overgrowth and a lot of bacterial imbalances in my gut. This discovery finally led me to the answers I had been searching for! I began to change my lifestyle by eating a whole foods-based diet, eliminating processed foods and added sugars, managing my stress, and taking specific supplements which quickly fixed my gut issues.

Right before I made this monumental discovery about my desired career path, I had applied and was accepted to pharmacy school. And to be completely honest, I was starting to regret even applying to pharmacy school. I originally applied to pharmacy school because I was curious about medications, and knew I'd be learning the chemistry side of how they worked in the body. I wanted to understand why people are on medications and be that person others can go to with any questions about their own medications. My friend at the time, who was also a chemistry major, told me that she had made the decision to apply to pharmacy school. I honestly thought this was all that I was able to do as a chemistry major and decided to follow her path. I remember telling my mom that I thought I was making the wrong decision. I asked myself, "Why am I about to go through pharmacy school when my passion is in functional medicine and holistic health/wellness?" I felt like I was signing up to do the exact opposite of what I was meant to do.

All of a sudden, it hit me. I thought about how there is a huge disconnect between Western Medicine and Eastern/Functional Medicine. I realized I needed to be a voice for the future doctors and pharmacists who could help make a lasting impact in the lives of their patients by helping them change their diets and lifestyle. It is crucial that future doctors and pharmacists understand how specific supplements, diet, and lifestyle changes are the foundation of lasting health. People go straight to medications to soothe the symptoms when something is wrong, but what about getting to the root cause? For example, let's say a patient has type 2 diabetes and the first solution they are offered is metformin, an oral medication to decrease hepatic glucose production. Evidence shows that type 2 diabetes is reversible, so why isn't the first solution the patient is offered education on reversing their disease, rather than just masking their symptoms?

I want to mention that I am not against all medications. There is a time and place for them, but they are being abused and prescribed more than necessary. I went to pharmacy school to learn about medications, their mechanism of action, their uses, side effects, and why people might be taking them. Ultimately, I am so thankful that I stuck with pharmacy school so that I could learn both aspects of medicine. I now understand why they are needed in some cases, however, I also learned more about their side effects and how much damage can be caused by not treating the root cause leading to further health complications.

Pharmacy school taught me a lot, but I was honestly shocked at how outdated and minimal the diet and lifestyle education are. In my experience, I took a one-hour course about nutrition and lifestyle habits in the entire 4 years I was there. That is insane! How are we supposed to be the future doctors when we aren't even taught the most simple and foundational forms of health? Changing our diet, eating real whole foods, looking at our toxic load, managing our stress, and lifestyle changes can prevent future health complications that are the leading causes of most diseases! We aren't taught any of this information in pharmacy school, and the majority of the information that we are taught about regarding diet and lifestyle, is outdated. I want to be the voice for future pharmacists, other pharmacy students, and other healthcare professionals.

Beginning My Journey with Functional Medicine

Future healthcare professionals need to understand how much our food, environment, toxins, and stress can impact long-term health.

All of these experiences and realizations are why I decided to create my own functional medicine practice. Having been through both digestive and hormonal issues for years, I realized that this is the area where I want to help people through my career. I also learned that through fixing my gut issues, eating more food, and exercising less, I was able to get my period back after stopping my birth control for a year. I could not believe that I was able to get my period back naturally without the help of a pill and by fixing the underlying issues. In the last four years I have dedicated my time to reading, researching, and experiencing all there is to know about the functional medicine style of practicing.

Because of my experience, knowledge, and training, in March 2021, when my skin started breaking out, I knew it had to be gut related. As I mentioned previously, your gut microbiome plays a huge role in various bodily functions, such as your skin health. When your skin reacts in such a way, it usually means something is going on internally. Having prior knowledge of functional medicine and understanding my body, I ordered myself a stool test. Not just any kind of stool test your normal physician may order for you, but a comprehensive one that takes a look at your good gut flora, bad gut flora, parasites, and tells you whether your organs are working properly through various lab markers. After ordering myself this test, I realized I had a prior infection causing my pancreas to stop making digestive enzymes. This means that anything I was eating wasn't being broken down and in turn, my face was breaking out. If I had just gone to a normal physician, they probably would have taken one look at my skin and told me to get on birth control or start medication of some kind. They definitely wouldn't ask about my diet or even wonder if my gut microbiome was optimal. This is another reason why I decided to start my own functional medicine practice and help others with their gut health, skin health, hormones, and any other health issues they may have. I want to be there for my patients every step of the way, advising them on diet, lifestyle, mental health, and more.

Normally, doctors won't order comprehensive stool analysis panels or certain lab values for whatever reason. The number of times I have tried to get past physicians to order cortisol level tests or full thyroid panels is outrageous. Anytime I asked them for certain labs, they told me my issues were not big enough for this type of testing. It took me seeing multiple doctors to even get through to them when wanting specific lab work done. Why would a physician deny their patient's requests when they should instead be listening to them? Physicians today typically spend a maximum of 15 minutes with their patients. This cannot be the future of medicine. Functional medicine is the future of medicine.

During pharmacy school, I worked at CVS Pharmacy as a Pharmacist Intern just to have a set job when I graduated. I worked every weekend, on top of attending pharmacy school five days a week. The work was draining me both mentally and physically. I felt like I was helping no one. The only things I was doing at work were filling prescriptions, counting medications, putting away new medications, and checking people out at the register. This was not fulfilling to me. Yes, I was counseling some patients on their new medications, but I couldn't help them with anything else. I knew that this was not something I wanted to do with my life, even if it was just a backup job for me post-graduation. I made the decision to quit after not even working there for a year. It wasn't for me. It wasn't bringing me the joy, passion, and lasting impact that I wanted in my career.

I knew that I wanted to have my own business of some sort in the future, but I never knew when it would happen. I was always hoping that someday, I would have my own Functional Medicine Practice, but

I was waiting for that "right time" and held myself back from thinking too much about it, for now. After leaving my Pharmacist Intern position at CVS, I realized there would never be a "right time." I had to go all in. This is something I am passionate about, and I want to start helping people *now* rather than "some day." Being able to work with various lab companies as a PharmD student and having the freedom to order any panels I want, is amazing. With the click of a button, I can have a full blood panel, cortisol level, full thyroid panel, hormone hair tests, a mold toxicity test, and even a comprehensive stool test ordered right away. This is a part of the medicine field where I can use my knowledge of functional medicine in order to help others with any issues they may have and order whatever tests they may need. I haven't even graduated with my Doctor of Pharmacy yet and I am already helping girls my age with their skin, hormonal, and gut issues. This is where I am supposed to be, and everything that I have experienced prior to this has led me to where I am today. I am eager to continue my journey into being the best Functional Medicine Practitioner and getting to the root cause of my clients' health issues. Having this knowledge of both Western and Eastern medicine is what will make me a leader in this industry for other pharmacists and other healthcare professionals. I want to change our current healthcare system into more of a treatment of the underlying cause, rather than masking symptoms with a pill. While medications will always be important in specific situations, we need to understand that they should not be what we run towards first when someone presents us with a health concern. It's time to get to the root cause and understand why someone might be having health issues in the first place.

I am so excited to announce that I have officially launched my functional medicine practice as a 4th year PharmD student, before I even graduate with my Doctor of Pharmacy! It's never too early or too late to do what you love to do. I have had a passion for functional medicine since I started understanding how to heal my own digestive and hormonal issues naturally with diet and lifestyle changes. I started looking at the root cause of my own issues, rather than continuing to "treat" them with a pill. Through my functional medicine journey, I found Dr. Christine Manukyan and saw that what she was doing with her life was exactly what I wanted to be doing with my life. When I graduate with my Doctor of Pharmacy in 2022, I will have already been helping others for almost a year! Dr. Christine took me under her wing as her intern through the Functional Medicine Business Academy, where I've learned the foundational skills needed to start my own business. She has guided me every step of the way and has pushed me to launch my website while still being a 4th year student still working on my rotations. I am so grateful to have a mentor like her to guide me through creating my functional medicine legacy. Through functional medicine, I will be helping so many people in the future with their digestive health, skin issues, hormonal issues, and more!

Sharing my journey, my struggles, and my passion for functional medicine will make me a better practitioner in the future. I am so excited to begin my journey in the medical profession in the functional medicine space. Having this background in Western medicine and experiencing the life-changing power of functional medicine will be a strong guide for me as I move forward into my practice. This is just the beginning for me! I never thought I would have the opportunity to be writing a book, but here we are. I have had one hell of a journey and I am thankful for this chance to share my functional medicine STORRIE™!

ABOUT KRISTINA TELHAMI

Kristina Telhami is a Certified Functional Medicine Specialist™ from Functional Medicine Business Academy™, Holistic Health Coach, and a PharmD Candidate. As the founder and CEO of *Top Health Solutions LLC*, she has worked with various young women struggling with digestive issues, hormonal imbalance, weight loss, and mindset through diet and lifestyle changes, as well as Functional Medicine lab testing.

After struggling with hormonal and digestive issues for years, Kristina healed her body through functional medicine practices, diet, and lifestyle changes. For the past four years, she has been researching, studying, and learning about holistic living and the importance of getting to the root cause of one's health issues.

Kristina has been featured on the Today Show, the Boost your biology podcast, and on the STORRIE™ podcast. She is passionate about helping others get to the root cause of their health issues and improve their quality of life holistically.

www.kristinatelhami.com | telhami.kristina@gmail.com | IG: @krissyt_pharmd

Chapter 12

A ROAD TO IKIGAI

By Krystyna Shepetiuk, PharmD, CDCES

"When you arise in the morning, think of what a precious privilege it is to be alive-to breathe, to think, to enjoy, to love."
– Marcus Aurelius

A beautiful sunset became part of my vision, when I first learned to truly dream. I picture myself standing on warm sand, watching the sunset, as I celebrate my 100th birthday, with a feeling of deep gratitude in my heart. This is vision casting, and this is what helps to propel me forward. I am extremely happy with my life, past, present and future. I am full of energy, life, and emotions. I laugh, dance, and travel. I continue to have dreams and set ambitious goals. I can go for long walks and hikes into the mountains. I salsa dance with my husband. I pick berries with my grandkids. I create my "blue zone of longevity" and expand the radius of the blue zone around me, while attracting hundreds of like-minded people, expanding this circle around the world. I know life is worth living when I can enjoy April showers, summer sunsets, autumn colors and the crunching of the snow in the winter. Life is worth the effort and sweat from the exercise, eating simple foods and continuously self-improving. I became the master of my life.

The Japanese people of Okinawa, have the secret to living a long, happy life. They have a unique purpose in life, their ikigai. It is described as the intersection of what you love and what you are good at. It is the place where, what the world needs and what you can get paid for, meet together. Ikigai gives you a reason for living, even when you are sad or miserable at the moment. It fosters resilience.

I have had my ikigai for a while now and want each and every one of you to have one also. I want this for you so you can be the CEO of your life and maximize your full potential. This does not require much from a single person. It comes down to the quality of small decisions that you make every day. Those small choices add up, they accumulate, they become big, and eventually, your life transforms. If each family, each country, and the entire world followed this movement, we could have a massive transformation.

A while back I wrote a letter to myself about courage, about belief in myself, about the fact that everyone is meant to live and have their unique mission, about the fact that everyone has a choice to create their extraordinary life. Each one of us knows that we have the capacity to achieve anything, but if we follow all of society's rules by going to school, college, and paying taxes, then why are we over-stressed and overworked? I often wondered, "How can I have it all?" How can I be so happy and fulfilled when I am trying to make a monthly house bill, school loan, car payment, and child expenses. Deep down, I felt I was not able to afford to think about these expensive thoughts.

My story towards finding my ikigai began when I was 29. I was an independent woman with a doctorate degree, dream job, and without a care in the world, well, maybe except for the school loans. I had no car payments, no rent, no monthly food expenses. I lived at home with my parents, I was comfortable, and honestly, I was getting sucked into society's fast-paced lifestyle. My drugs of choice were distraction, a heavy workload, and winning by climbing the corporate ladder.

Shortly after this time in my life, I met my husband, got married, and started a family. With these changes, my priorities started shifting. I delved into lifelong, deep questions about life's purpose, and whether I was at the "right" point in my life. I had a paradigm shift. I now had to think about a retirement plan, my kid's college funds, and most importantly, my own health. I was lost and disorganized with my "why." I was stressed and exhausted from balancing a new family life, and life as a manager. I was anxious and angry about the bills piling up on my kitchen counter. I often felt like I was living paycheck to paycheck. Feelings of uncertainty were giving me anxiety and fear on a daily basis. I was living a mediocre life, a societal rat race.

I attempted changing my life's trajectory and setting long term goals by making a vision board, watching the movie *The Secret*, having sticky notes of daily affirmations on my bathroom mirror, and working on self-development, but saw no significant results. Without even realizing, I was stuck in a hamster wheel. We were stuck. My husband gained an extra 30lbs and had started looking for different ways to lose it. I remember his disappointment when we went to Vail, Colorado, and the struggle he had to tie his snow boots. I saw even more disappointment when the phlebotomist came to do blood work for our life insurance plan and told him that he was in the "high-risk" category for life insurance. The real picture did not represent his, or my, vision for our future. In reality, we both wanted to eat healthy, look healthy, and feel healthy, but were getting different results despite our attempts. He then tried several other things including going to the gym every day, going on extreme diets, and even counting calories. Nothing was working as his weight just kept coming back.

This is when I started noticing other problems around me. I remember signing up my daughter for summer camp and being disappointed with the lunch menu which included pizza, hamburgers, hot dogs, and other low nutritional value foods. I was extremely disappointed that my kids were going to be exposed to all these impostor foods, with no benefits except to fill up their bellies.

In the Spring of 2019, my husband and I attended a Tony Robbins event which taught me that the best investment you could make is to invest in yourself. The most important lesson that I took away from this, was learning to adjust my mindset. In addition to that, I learned to understand that I am capable of anything I set my mind to, and that I am worth it, and I already have enough credibility to follow my passions. Walt Disney said it best, "If you can visualize it, if you can dream it, there's some way to do it."

Looking back to that day, I can say that it was during our stay at Tony's event, Unleash the Power Within (UPW), where my transformation began. I had a deep emotional experience that touched the most sensitive strings of my soul. It exposed me, made me defenseless, left me alone, with no one but myself. I talked to myself, got to know myself, opened up to myself. I cried, laughed, and experienced many emotions in a short period of time. I stood face-to-face with my gigantic fears, which hung over my head, as if they wanted to attack and devour me, but my faith in myself, my strength, which I felt in every part of my being, enveloped me in the light of my inner strength, and did not give my fears any chance. My fears left me. My limiting beliefs were transformed into beliefs that eventually changed my thinking.

As I was standing in the crowd with 35,000 people, I was waiting for my turn to finally overcome my fears. I was ready to finally master my uncontrollable energy that often overwhelmed me. I asked myself, "How is this possible? What does this mean to me?" As I got to the front of the line, in front of me was a bed of hot coals at 1,000 degrees Fahrenheit, and I was being challenged to walk across it. At this point, the fear was gone and instead there was a sense of confidence and excitement accompanied by the support of all the like-minded people going through this with me. It was unreal. I repeated to myself, "Yes! Yes! Yes! I am ready. Yes, I can. Yes, I am strong. Yes, I am the master of my life." I stood tall and straight, in a wonder woman pose, repeating "cool moss" as I marched across 20 feet of coals representing all of life's challenges and obstacles. I was overcoming my fears and insecurities. I knew that by replacing negative emotions with positive ones, I could get through anything. The exercise taught me to understand Tony's favorite line, "Where focus goes, energy flows."

During my time with Tony, I wanted to have it all. I wanted to have balance in all the important areas of my life. I had the burning passion to become a better version of me, to become the Master of Health to help my family, the world, and myself. What I took away from that event was that health and fitness are the foundational categories that I had to take charge over, because there is not a single area of life that health and fitness does not affect. It sets the stage for success. I decided to use the health and fitness category as leverage to become better in other areas like parenting, my love relationship, career, financial life, intellectual intelligence, spiritual life, and emotional capacity. My purpose became very clear. I knew I wanted to feel energized into my old age, to be able to salsa dance into my 80's or even 100's. Or be able to go hiking and skiing with my grandkids.

I knew something had to change. Our birth is a miracle. After listening to a TED Talk by Mel Robbins where she said, "You are one in a trillion," I knew I was meant to do more. I was given an opportunity to have a life, to have a mission so that I can change my life, and ultimately, the world. I decided to prioritize my health because I wanted to feel "enough." I wanted to be enough for myself, and my family. What I wanted for them is what I wanted for myself, and thus, I started walking the walk, and setting an example for my family first.

As I was going through my personal transformation, I started evaluating other important areas of my own life. There is so much more to lifestyle transformation than food choices. There is also mindset, movement, muscle load, sleep, energy, our genes, the environment we live in, and different toxins we are exposed to. I remember back in pharmacy school, one of my professors telling my class, "You will be on the front line of medicine, because prevention is key." At the time, I was questioning his thinking, because to me, I was in pharmacy school, and I was just supposed to counsel on medication safety. For some reason, though, I believed him, and his words stayed on my long-term memory shelf. While being a medication expert is important. At that moment, I understood more than ever that medication use should come secondary to lifestyle modifications, at least in the ambulatory setting. Healthcare professionals should be partnering with their client in a relationship, keeping them accountable, and helping them be the CEOs of their life, and not just hand out a prescription upon request. It is so easy to put a bandage on a problem in the form of medication, because it's convenient and it gives you a quick solution. However, finding the root cause of the problem, and fixing the problem from within, is where you will get the most return on investment in the long run.

Although my husband looked healthy and normal to me, his disappointment propelled me into action. I had to take action. I started researching and came across a short book called, *Eat, Stop, Eat* written by Brad Pilion, that I read while back in pharmacy school and had some experience with. I also found a more recent article from New England Journal of Medicine (NEJM) on intermittent fasting titled, "Effects of Intermittent Fasting on Health, Aging, and Disease." Like most men, my husband likes results, and the NEJM review article really inspired him to try yet another recipe. Later on, we watched *Food Inc.* on Netflix and started to re-evaluate our family lifestyle habits.

With this new awakening, I knew that I wanted my kids to be exposed to real foods, to eat the kinds of foods I ate as a child, until age 11, as I grew up in Ukraine. My favorite sweet treats consisted of berries we picked in the forest, homegrown strawberries, gooseberries, red and black currant, cherries, apples, pears, plums. We had a homemade cake a few times a year during major holidays, as our budget allowed. Every Sunday, I remember picking mushrooms with my dad, and later my mom, and making the best meals. We had our own chickens, ducks, goats and a cow. We even had our own orchard. We did not have processed foods. We also practiced regenerative farming. Thinking back, every family had a full abundance of true organic products, however, with modernization and progress worldwide, most people became addicted to processed foods and sugar.

At home, healing from within became my go-to therapy, instead of my medicine cabinet.

I started using food as medicine, incorporating the rainbow of foods on each plate, adding prebiotic foods like asparagus, chicory root, and probiotic foods like sauerkraut. We used pineapple at the onset of a fever and used anti-inflammatory herbs such as turmeric to create an autophagy enhancer tea, made of herbs. The language in my house changed. My 3 and 5-year-old started distinguishing junk foods with low nutritional value, from healthy foods with high nutritional value. They would discuss it in school, at their grandparent's house, and among other kids of the same age. Our thinking changed. I stopped thinking about what others around me want and do, and instead, focused on what I want. I wanted to know more.

I started to become obsessed with functional medicine, holistic wellness approaches, and biohacking your own biology. This inspired me to enroll into a functional medicine program. I started educating myself on nutrition, became certified in diabetes care, and became an education specialist. I also enrolled into a nutrigenomics certificate program, in order to understand interactions between genes and diet.

With the help of functional medicine and biohacking, my husband was the first person I helped to achieve the massive health transformation he had always been searching for. We started with mindset setting, then changing our food choices, and picked up intermittent fasting (eating during an 8-hour window). We also began doing a biohacking exercise through HIIT, tracking sleep, morning cold therapy exposure, and breath work. If you think about our body, it is all interconnected, our organs, cells, neurons are communicating and collaborating constantly. Therefore, our body needs to be looked at holistically.

Through intermittent fasting, you can train your body to get rid of excess fat by tapping into the body's fat reserve, and as a result, getting an incredible amount of energy and health. My old belief of having 3 meals per day was changed to understanding that our bodies need rest, and it cannot get it if it's constantly working on the digestion process. You can train your body to eat less. According to the culture on Okinawa Island in Japan, the practice of "hara hachi bu" is to stop eating when your stomach is 80% full. My old belief of eating everything off your plate, was changed to, instead, practice mindful eating. We need to be present with our meal without distractions such as phones or TV. The pandemic was a great time to practice mindfulness. I asked my husband to join me in a challenge of eating one meal per day for one month, in order to really learn to appreciate the food. We completed this challenge in the summer of 2020. Although it was not easy to get used to, I learned of ways to bio hack this process, and to make it easier. To decrease stress and anxiety around perceived hunger, having a system helped so much. Changing things like having a morning and bedtime routine, having a meal plan, drinking bulletproof coffee in the morning, drinking plenty of water, especially when starting to feel hunger, and finally, staying busy.

Through this holistic approach, my husband was able to release his extra weight and keep it off. Once again, he was confident enough to live the life he envisioned, to be the role model for our kids without having a big belly, to no longer be at high risk for chronic diseases, and most importantly, he became the owner of his own choices. He had the power to decide what foods he ate and became the owner of his habits. Our oldest daughter was no longer teasing him about having "a balcony," or a big tummy. He was running a new life. We, as a family, were creating a new life. We created a family constitution and chose to be the CEOs of our own life. This was not a diet, it was a lifestyle change, a mindset change. It transformed our health. The mindset transformation took about 90 days and did not stop there. We started to be more aware of what we are putting in our mouth, our brain, our energy, our sleep, our movement. We started to bio hack our entire body. I started to reprogram my brain to only want the things that are healthy for my body. This also made me think of another limiting belief. The belief of exercising to be able to eat what I want. In reality, that does not work. Your body deserves quality foods to start exercising and performing at the maximum potential.

Over the pandemic, I went through many self-reflecting moments, and really focused on my true ikigai. I knew it was up to me to take that first step, to take my experience and put it to practice. Although my background is to be a medication expert, my passion is holistic wellness. Finding the root cause of the problem, using food as medicine, maximizing the body's potential through preventative care, and biohacking your biology to age backwards, led me to believe that pharmaceuticals should only be used as a last resort. Biohacking, as I learned more in the past couple of years, is a way to make your biology more polished like a diamond. Biohacking helps transform your body to feel and be the best version it can be, with each new day.

Now, more than ever, I understand that we are living in a world of food products that are impostors. With different flavors such as bacon, cheese, and chili, that are full of carbohydrates and unnatural fats for the human body. Once this processed food touches our tongue receptors, it tricks our body, and in the midst of the sedentary lifestyle, this leads to increased fat production. This leaves us hungry, causing overeating and increased chances for chronic diseases, such as diabetes. Connecting functional medicine, along with biohacking and analysis of your genetic code, creates miracle solutions. You can gain more energy and maximize your body's full potential. Most people go to traditional doctors when they have a problem to fix, but taking care of your body holistically, from a young age, can help prevent many of the future problems, and most importantly, creates an extraordinary lifestyle.

Besides physical health, my mind needed to be healthy. The exercises available for this are gratitude and meditation. They helped with finding my way in the dark towards internal peace, and entering the state of consciousness, all while understanding the fact that life is not a random occurrence. Life is not a destiny written by someone above, instead, it is a series of consequences for our own decisions. The law of cause and effect is a universal law. I started practicing appreciation by journaling every morning and night. As a family, we started practicing gratitude with kids during dinner time and having meaningful conversations. I started showing gratitude for the simplest things, like, "I am grateful for being able to watch you practice gymnastics today." My son, Will, said, "I am grateful for having a happy day today." My kids started fighting with each about who goes first in saying their gratitude. This practice helped me feel good about myself, about my life, and more importantly, I started seeing positive changes happening around me. I started getting more opportunities at work, I connected with other like-minded health care professionals that care about functional medicine, and truly began healing from within. I started receiving business opportunities to work with medical doctors to launch start-up businesses. Opportunities kept coming in mysterious ways. I was attracting opportunities in abundance. I trained my mind to appreciate things, to establish a flow through me, with blessings and grace, and with ease. I started noticing that this mindset was helping me to eliminate my stress and anxiety around "having it all." What you appreciate, appreciates. When you are fully giving it all every day, it comes back to you. Crafting your ideal life is a life-long project, because life is not a marathon. I found my true ikigai, and I am in the right moment in my life, to change the world.

While functional medicine made me look into the root cause of the real issue at hand, biohacking made me more curious, strengthened my willpower and endurance, and helped me to balance my life. I am super excited about the future! I feel like a superhuman with each and every day. My metabolic age is younger than my chronological age. Every day, I see and feel changes, and I understand my body much better. I am extremely excited about nutrigenomics and epigenetics and their power to help people prevent modern chronic diseases. As a pharmacist, I am excited about helping people find an individualized prescription plan that works for their body. In addition, more cutting-edge biohacking principles, like nootropics, neurofeedback, heart rate variability training, and more.

I am confident that we are all healthy to some extent. Our health is not defined as one single marker, instead, it comprises all of our genetics, metabolic pathways, emotional state, and social state. While we can have lower quality markers in one area, others may have higher quality. Each of us has a unique health map. Through my new established LLC, *BioX Unlimited*™, I can now help clients maximize their good markers, and improve their weaker ones, all within six months. I work with clients through an individualized approach, by combining functional medicine, biohacking, and your genetics. Once a client decides to work with me, I start with a nutrigenomics test, which is a blueprint to help understand how individual genetics can help each one of us, individually. Based on the individual DNA, you have a unique opportunity to have immediate recommendations and actions to work on, in order to elevate your health. To further enhance your health, I would dive deeper into other functional tests, such as a food sensitivity test, hormone test, metal toxicity test, and overall nutritional evaluation.

Although the definition of biohacking was added to the Webster dictionary, it can be described differently. Is it philosophy or is it technology? I believe that it is a combination of philosophy, technology, and lifestyle. Starting today, you can also start biohacking your health and having a higher quality of life. Start with having a bedtime routine and going to sleep at the same time every day. Practice gratitude every morning or in the evening. Move your body every day and incorporate HIIT exercise 2-3x per week. Expose yourself to cold showers, which is linked to improved quality sleep, leading to more focus, and even an improved immune system. Spend more time in nature and get extra points for being surrounded by evergreen trees, which are known to help boost your own natural killer cells and enhance your immune system. I invite you to have a chat with me about intermittent fasting, the power of gratitude, or increasing sleep quality. Download my favorite mobile apps *Simple* for intermittent fasting, *Pillow* to track your sleep, and *Wim Hof* for breathwork exercises. Remember that you are 1 in a trillion, and you were meant to do more on this planet.

May each of you be diligent and live in harmony with yourself and the world around you. May your "north star" show you the way to your dreams and may each of you enjoy your family, your work, your occupation, and every moment of your life. Each of you can and should be the CEO of your life and make the most of your potential. There is no success without effort, but through conscious actions you can have an extraordinary life! My children became my why, my health became my leverage and my passion for functional medicine, biohacking, and nutrigenetics became my life's purpose and mission. Are you ready to discover yours?

ABOUT DR. KRYSTYNA SHEPETIUK

Dr. Krystyna Shepetiuk aka Dr. Kryss is a Certified Functional Medicine Specialist™ from Functional Medicine Business Academy™, diabetes coach, biohacker and firewalker. Dr. Krystyna is a busy mother of three and the founder and CEO of BioX Unlimited. While building her online functional medicine practice, she works as a Clinical Pharmacist with a Pharmacy Benefit Manager (PBM). As an overwhelmed and overworked mother of three, Dr. Krystyna worked hard to transform her own life and mindset through Tony Robbins' programs and made the decision to help others create their way to an extraordinary life through functional medicine, biohacking, and nutrigenomics.

Dr. Krystyna believes that managing your health is a life-long journey and soulful project. She believes that you can elevate your health to the next level through the quality of small everyday decisions, life "hacks", and altering your own biology. Through consistency, diligence, and discipline, anyone can change their lives. Dr. Krystyna is an expert in mindset coaching, habit and productivity building. Her specialties are focused around sleep, intermittent fasting, longevity, and nutrigenomics.

Dr. Krystyna is on a mission to create blue zone communities, and she believes that it all starts at home. Together with her husband, they have created a unique wellness home philosophy and teach their kids and clients about food as medicine, exercise, meditation, sleep and the power of gratitude. She believes that human potential is unlimited, and she wants others to fine-tune their life in the most important areas in order to achieve optimal health and lives altogether.

www.drkryss.com | hello@drkryss.com | IG: @drkryss

Chapter 13

LIVING LIFE ON YOUR TERMS

By Lisette Miranda Alba, PharmD, BS

"There is no greater thing you can do with your life and your work than follow your passions in a way that serves the world and you."

– Richard Branson.

It's truly incredible what you can create when you focus on your *why*. I have been on many paths over the last 8 years that have converged into one path, evolving into one long journey that has brought me to where I am today. In this chapter, you will not only get to know a little about me and why I've decided to embark on this journey, but you will also learn how I arrived to where I am today.

This whole journey starts with my passion for teaching. Since I was a little girl, I created a classroom in my bedroom and pretended my dolls and stuffed animals were my students. As I grew older, I tutored my friends or classmates who were struggling in school and was even referred by family and friends to tutor a few other younger students. I truly enjoyed sharing my knowledge and helping others become successful in areas in which they were struggling. Throughout my whole childhood and halfway through high school, I always thought I would pursue teaching as a career. Teaching is obviously a huge passion of mine, but so is learning. I love learning about things that interest me, and as you continue reading, you will learn more about those interests. There is no better teacher than the one that never stops learning.

So how did I go from wanting to become a teacher to becoming a pharmacist? Well, when I was in 10th grade, in the year 2000, one of my cousins asked me what my plans were after high school. I told her, "I am going to be a teacher." There was never a doubt in my mind that teaching was the perfect career choice for me. I loved teaching, but I also knew at the time that I wanted to raise a family and be an attentive mother. I was lucky enough to always have a parent at home until I was 10 years old. I wanted to provide that for my own future family in some way. Besides, what other career do you know that has summers off? The summer I was turning 14, I was hired by my mother's boss to do clerical work at a private vehicle tag agency, and this was my very first job. I worked throughout high school every day after school and on Saturdays with my mom. I am so grateful that I was able to spend all those years working next to her.

My cousin, who was 10 years my senior and had experience working in the health field, suggested I look into pharmacy as a career. My cousin told me, "There's a demand for pharmacists." Ironically, I had an open topic English paper to write, so I decided to take advantage and do some research on careers in pharmacy. I fell in love with the diversity of jobs, choosing pharmacy as a profession. Writing that 10-page paper gave me a whole new perspective on the possibility of earning a degree in a well-paid career and actually becoming a doctor! There were so many specialties and potential jobs to choose within the pharmacy field. On top of that, I could still teach as a professor, if I decided to pursue that path. Thus, I shifted gears and started working on getting into pharmacy school. I started volunteering at local hospital pharmacies and shadowed at a local independent pharmacy my family frequently visited. I learned what it was like to be in the field and interviewed pharmacists along the way. I started taking college classes, while in high school, that were prerequisites for pharmacy school. Before graduating from high school, I applied to the Dual Enrollment Pharmacy Program at Nova Southeastern University (NSU) in Davie, FL and was accepted with a scholarship for the undergrad program. I was so proud of this accomplishment.

Throughout my school years, I always strived to get the best grades possible. I earned straight As on all my report cards. When I didn't earn an A, it struck a nerve. I'm not writing this here to brag, but to share that I'm a hard worker and I don't do anything half-heartedly. Some things came easy to me, but there were others for which I actually had to study a little harder. My best subjects were always Math and Science. I'll never forget my second semester of undergrad at NSU. I was taking both General Chemistry I and Trigonometry, back-to-back. I literally ran out of the chemistry class to get to the math class. I was so focused on acing chemistry, that I let my confidence get the best of me in my trigonometry class, until I got a C in the class! It was then that I knew I had to strategize my studying methods if I wanted to keep up my good grades. I started paying equal attention to both classes and managed to pass both with an A.

After two years of undergrad, I started my pharmacy school adventure in 2004. I was fascinated with learning about medications and how they worked within the body. The summer after my first year of pharmacy school, I started interning at the 3-letter pharmacy chain. There I was balancing pharmacy school, my social life, and two part-time jobs. Yes, you read that right, two jobs! One was the retail pharmacy and the other was the tag agency I started working at in high school. I went in to work at the tag agency only on Saturdays and worked one weeknight at the retail pharmacy after class. I really wanted to start working in the pharmacy world as soon as possible in order to start gaining experience. So, I managed to work at both places, keep up my grades and have a social life.

As you can tell by now, I stay busy. When I wasn't in class, I was either working, studying, going to the gym, or having fun with my friends and then boyfriend (now husband). I joined clubs in school and participated in lots of events. You could say I am a social butterfly, which is to be expected as I was born on the Cancer/Leo cusp. I love connecting with people and creating meaningful relationships. Everywhere I go, I start a conversation, make a connection and sometimes even create new friendships. Working in a retail pharmacy requires a special type of person with a great personality, and I believe anyone working in retail can validate this statement. I honestly love working in retail and developing relationships with my coworkers and my patients. Now, just because I love it doesn't mean I don't recognize that it is a highly stressful job and that there are many rough days. This stress eventually caught up with me.

I'm going to fast-forward to May 2008. I had graduated from pharmacy school and was newlywed. I was excited to start working and to get my life started with my husband. After applying to several companies, I decided to accept the offer from the company with which I interned. During my first few years as a pharmacist, I worked in both retail and hospital pharmacy, do you see the pattern here? Two jobs again! Then in 2010, I was blessed to become the mother of a beautiful princess, and this was the highlight of my life. I had always dreamed of becoming a mom and raising a family. Being a mother is quite literally a full-time job, so by now, I technically had 3 jobs. Shortly after becoming a mom, I decided to resign from my job at the hospital but continued working retail. I wanted to spend more time at home with my daughter. My family has always been my priority. In 2013, I was blessed with another pregnancy, another little girl. Now this is where it starts to get interesting. Early in the pregnancy, I had an unexpected inflammation develop in one of my toe joints. Luckily, it was not painful, but I could not figure out how to treat the inflammation. My daughter was born in November 2013, and in January 2014, I started on my journey to figure out what was wrong with my health.

2014 was a pivotal year in my life. So many things happened in so many areas of my life that could have scarred me, but I came out resilient. If they gave an award for surviving a bad year, I'm sure that would have been the year I won. I took advantage of my maternity leave in early 2014 by scheduling a doctor's appointment with an orthopedic specialist. A normal X-ray only created more curiosity that led to an MRI. The MRI revealed my inflammation but raised even more questions about a possible diagnosis. I was referred to another orthopedic doctor, who took another X-ray, which revealed bone damage. How was this possible?! It had only been two months since the last X-ray, and that one was supposedly "normal." After all the doctor visits, scans and referrals, I finally visited a rheumatologist in March. The blood work the rheumatologist ordered didn't confirm anything, so my condition was still a mystery. At this time, my maternity leave was over, and I had to get back to work. Returning to a stressful work environment, having two kids under 4, and not knowing what was wrong with me was very disruptive for me both mentally and physically. This is when new symptoms started to show up as well. I had pain and stiffness in every single joint of my body. Simple daily tasks like getting out of bed, answering the telephone at work and going up the stairs were a struggle. I was taking anti-inflammatory medication and muscle relaxers around-the-clock just to be able to function and go to work. This was a very devastating point in my life. There were days that the pain and stiffness were so bad that I cried because I didn't know how to deal with it. I am grateful that my babies were easy to care for and that my husband and father were there to support me through this difficult time. Without them, I don't know how I would have surpassed my worst days. Honestly, my children were the driving force that kept me motivated to want to recover my health.

After a while, I returned to the rheumatologist, and they still didn't have an explanation for my mysterious inflammation in the one toe joint or any of my new symptoms. It was definitive that I needed surgery to repair the bone damage, so he referred me back to the orthopedic surgeon and requested a biopsy. At this point, the doctor was just trying to rule out any other possibilities. By mid-May, I returned to the surgeon to schedule my surgery. He had me get a new X-ray, and this time, the bone damage was even worse! As I sat in the room waiting for the doctor to come in, I looked at the X-ray and thought to myself, he's going to come in here and tell me that this could be cancer! Sure enough, about 5-10 minutes later, the doctor walks in, sits down and says, "You know, I have to tell you that this could be cancer." He stated that the fact that the damage was getting worse at such an accelerated rate could imply it was cancer. We proceeded to schedule my surgery for the following week, but he wanted me to get another opinion from the only Orthopedic Oncologist in South Florida. I kept my composure until I walked out of the building. Once outside, I broke down into tears and called my dad. I cried all the way home, devastated, thinking about the worst-case scenario. What's going to happen to my family if this really is cancer? My biggest fear was leaving my girls behind without a mother and leaving my husband in financial distress.

Thankfully, I was able to see the specialist that same week. He reviewed my case, did an ultrasound, and said he didn't believe I had cancer. What a relief! He said that the excessive, untreated synovitis, an inflammation of the synovium (connective tissue) around the joint, was the cause of the bone damage. The specialist performed my foot surgery the following week. Now, remember, at the time, I was still working as a retail pharmacist, so now I had to take another month off to recover. This time I was on crutches and in a boot for one month. During this time, the results of the biopsy taken from the surgery came back. They revealed... nothing! Apparently, I just had this strange inflammation that came from nowhere and caused pain, stiffness and bone damage, therefore, based on symptoms and lack of evidence of anything else, I was diagnosed with seronegative Rheumatoid Arthritis (RA). As a pharmacist, I had never heard of this, so I started researching. My body seems to have arthritis, but there is no evidence in the blood work, no rheumatoid factors, no antibodies, nada. In contrast, when diagnosed with seropositive RA, you have antibodies that attack your body and cause inflammation in your joints. Retrospectively, my husband and I came to the conclusion that my RA is probably related to my Lyme Disease diagnosis. I bet you were not expecting that twist. I was diagnosed with Lyme in late 2011, two years after being bitten by a tick. I was treated for it and completely forgot about it, until this all started happening. I live in Florida, so the last thing that crossed my mind was the possibility of getting Lyme. It has never been confirmed that my RA is related to Lyme, but I am almost certain it is. After all, it would be a logical explanation. According to healthline.com, Lyme can be a risk factor for developing RA and other forms of arthritis. Some people develop post-Lyme arthritis even after being treated for Lyme with antibiotics.

The treatment for seronegative RA and seropositive RA is the same. Both are treated with non-steroidal anti-inflammatory drugs (NSAIDs), muscle relaxers, and biologics. I did not look forward to a lifetime of having to take any of these medications, especially considering the potential side effects and immunosuppression. I took some time to continue researching while recovering from my surgery and tried to figure out what I could do for myself. Once I was cleared to start exercising after the surgery, I realized that my right leg was really weak. The muscles had deteriorated, and the toe joint that was repaired had absolutely no flexibility. I couldn't even do a lunge. I was still overweight from the pregnancy and was determined to get back in shape. I did some more research and found that yoga is one of the best exercises for RA patients. I turned to the wonderful world of YouTube and started doing yoga at home. I fell in love with yoga and what it did for my body. There was a period in my life where I did yoga every day, and sometimes multiple times a day. Yoga was not only providing my body with the strength and flexibility that it needed to protect my joints but was also helping me manage my stress. I talked about yoga to everyone. I went to a few classes in my community and had my friends join me for yoga classes.

In addition to finding the right exercises for my health condition, I knew that my nutrition was also an important part in order to maintain my health long term. I started researching the difference between inflammatory foods and anti-inflammatory foods. I learned about natural herbs, supplements and essential oils that could be used to help manage my inflammation. I began taking supplements and natural herbs to improve the health of my joints. I started using essential oils to boost my immune system, detox my body and treat any intermittent flare-ups. My parents always trusted alternative remedies and believed in their ability to cure diseases, and so did I. Over the years, all these lifestyle changes have helped me lose weight, gain strength and flexibility, have more energy and keep my RA in remission without taking medications. You read that right, without medications! Now, I want you to realize I did this on my own. My doctors did not recommend lifestyle changes. They encouraged it and were happy to see me doing well and thriving, but all they did was prescribe medications and see me every 3 months to do blood work and check my joints. As a pharmacist, I could have very well trusted my doctor, followed instructions, and taken the medications as prescribed, but my intuition told me otherwise. My doctor is well aware of how I manage my disease and knows that I am not using my medications as prescribed. To this day, I never miss my rheumatology visits because I want to make sure what I am doing is working and that I am in control of my disease. When the pandemic started, my RA had been in remission for a long time and my doctor, and I agreed that it would be wise to suspend using immunosuppressant medications.

The year 2020 was an unforgettable year for all of us, but for me, it was also a year of personal growth. My health was on track. I was still learning about better ways to continue improving my health holistically. I became interested in the use of essential oils and became more aware of toxins in common household products most people use daily. I decided to create my own collection of oils and learned how to use them to improve the health and wellness of my family and me. I began switching out toxic products we used daily for non-toxic ones. As I was diving deeper into my holistic health journey, I realized that something was still missing. My life was chaotic. I was still working in a stressful environment. Financially, I wasn't struggling, but I yearned to be in a better place. Although I seemed to be managing everything well on the outside, on the inside I was a ball of frustration. I was unsatisfied with my life. I had so many dreams and goals that I wanted to accomplish, and I had no idea how I was going to make them happen. I started searching for different business-related ideas and instead found a mindset program called *"Wake Up with Joy."* I invested in myself and committed to this 8-week program in February

2020. This program changed how I viewed myself and my life. It helped me to realize that I had already accomplished so much more than other people had, and that I was doing amazingly well for myself. My renewed mindset sparked something that I had forgotten about, my passion for teaching. This was the moment I decided I wanted to become a certified yoga teacher to share my love and knowledge of yoga with the world. Why stop there? I found this whole new world of essential oils, which I was fascinated by, and wanted to share with others! I had no idea how I was going to do this, but I knew that was the direction I was choosing to go.

At this time my amazing friend, Phi Delta Chi "big brother", and colleague, Dr. Christine Manukyan, had just launched her own virtual functional medicine practice. I had no idea what that was or what she was doing, but I was intrigued. One day, we connected on the phone and when she explained to me what functional medicine was, my mind was blown! I thought to myself, "This is it! This is what I've been looking for!" I had been practicing functional medicine on myself all along, not realizing exactly what I was doing for the previous 6 years. When Dr. Christine told me she was going to start the *Functional Medicine Business Academy*™ to teach other pharmacists how to start their own practice, I knew I could not let this opportunity pass. The time to take action came in March 2021. I started her mini course and within 3 months, I launched my own practice! I can't believe how much my life has changed since I made the decision to invest in myself and create my own business. I had two big reasons: my health and my family. I knew that if I continued to work in a stressful environment, I would continue to risk having another relapse.

Ultimately, I had been searching for a way to generate an income and be home with my girls and my husband. Having my own virtual functional medicine practice was the perfect solution to be able to live out my passion. I am able to teach other women struggling with stress and chronic health conditions how to overcome those burdens holistically and live joyfully. I officially launched my practice June 8th, 2021, and I couldn't be happier. Since launching my practice, I have helped many women discover the root causes of their ailments and have helped them heal their bodies without medications. I have educated many people about the benefits of yoga, meditation, detox, and using essential oils in their daily life. I have been able to spend more time with my family and generate an income from the comfort of my own home. It has been one hell of a ride, and I am only getting started! I can't wait to see what the future will bring! If you resonate with any part of my story, I encourage you to listen to your gut and make a decision to live your life on your terms.

ABOUT DR. LISETTE ALBA

Dr. Lisette Alba is a Certified Functional Medicine Specialist™ from Functional Medicine Business Academy™, Holistic Health and Mindset Coach, Essential Oils Educator, and Certified Medication Therapy Management (MTM) Pharmacist. She is a dedicated wife and mother of two beautiful young girls. Dr. Alba is the CEO and Founder of her own virtual Functional Medicine Practice, *Holistic Simple Living, LLC*. Dr. Lisette's practice specializes in helping stressed-out women achieve their health and wellness goals with holistic lifestyle changes so they can create their ideal and balanced life.

Prior to entering the world of functional medicine and launching her own practice, she spent 13 years working as a Community and Clinical Pharmacist with various leadership roles. During her own struggle with an autoimmune disease and chronic stress, Dr. Lisette took control of her health and educated herself in the holistic healing effects of yoga, meditation, and essential oils. Dr. Lisette is currently pursuing a certification to become a Certified Yoga Teacher in order to deepen her knowledge of yoga and share its benefits with her clients. She also discovered the importance of stress management and the power of a positive mindset. Dr. Lisette used this knowledge to heal her own body and regain control of her health, without medications. During this holistic health journey, she found her calling in empowering other women to regain control of their life and health by using a simple, holistic approach.

Dr. Lisette is a frequent speaker on the therapeutic effects of essential oils, adopting a toxic-free lifestyle, managing stress, and reducing inflammation. She has been featured on the STORRIE™ Podcast, the Balanced Wellness Solutions Podcast, and The Gaby U Show, and on The Gaby U YouTube channel.

Dr. Lisette is passionate about teaching overwhelmed, busy women how to reclaim their lives and health by guiding them through a simple holistic transformation. This transformation teaches them to manage their stress, change their mindset, and find the root cause of their health issues all through her specialized testing, personalized protocols and recommendations, and her one-of-a-kind coaching program.

www.drlisettealba.com | dr.lisettealba@gmail.com | IG: @dr.lisettealba

Chapter 14

TAKING CHARGE OF OUR HEALTH

By Marlene Nanda Rosana FNP-C, DNP

"Your journey is completely yours. It is unique. Others may try to steal part of it, tell it in their words or shape it to suit them. Reality is, no one can live it or own it but you. Take charge of your journey, it's yours and yours alone!"

– Kemi Sogunle

"There is nothing you can do about it! You just have to learn how to manage!" As I heard these words coming from my son's pediatrician, and I was trying to let them sink in, I felt a pain in my flesh. I was trying to comprehend what the doctor meant. Yes, I was a nurse and yes, I had taken care of several patients with breathing issues, and allergies, but this was my son he was talking about. This was our first son, Tyivon, the joy of our lives. He was just 12 months old. He was just a baby, and I couldn't help but wonder how his life would be if he was already having severe allergic reactions. This sweet, little boy that I had brought into this world, was allergic to eggs, almonds, cashew, fish, walnuts, pecans, cat, pollen, and the list goes on. Poor baby. On top of that, he had issues with eczema, constipation, seasonal allergies, wheezing, and was an extremely picky eater. I couldn't help but wonder if it was my fault. But before I jump ahead of myself, let me start from the beginning.

I moved from Cameroon, Central Africa, to the United States in December 1999. I was 20 years old and had big dreams. My plan was to become a doctor and then return to Cameroon, where I was planning on opening small clinics to help the poor communities. Of course, life didn't go as planned. Upon arriving in the United States, I quickly convinced myself that medical school would be very hard to get into as an international student. It was also just too expensive, and there was no way my parents could afford it. I followed the advice of the international student advisor, and the Dean of Nursing at the community college I was in and enrolled in nursing school instead. After all, I would still be able to help people like I always wanted to do. I relished going to nursing school and graduated with my associate degree. Then, my plan was to enroll back in school to get my bachelor's degree in nursing but, online this time. Then, September 11th happened, and all international students were prohibited from taking online classes. It was too late for me to find another school, and I ended up losing my international student status. For about 2 years, I started working as a registered nurse in Olathe, Kansas. It is important to remember that life is not always going to take you in a straight path. Always be ready for the unexpected. Jason Silva alludes to this by stating that, "There's always going to be the circumstances you can't plan for. There's always the unexpected relevance and the serendipity."

In 2005, a friend of mine told me about a lawyer who could help me obtain my green card due to the nationwide shortage of nurses. That's exactly what I did. But the only condition for me was to return to Cameroon and go to an appointment at the American embassy. I was scared, because there was a possibility of my petition getting denied and me being stuck in Cameroon. I made up my mind and decided to take that leap of faith. People around me did not understand my decision and were advising me against it. They were telling me to, "advance in my academia," or that "I need to file for a green card that will allow me to be accepted in school." Hence, I chose to trust God instead. I went home for the Green Card application. During my medical exam in Cameroon, I found out that I had uterine fibroids. Fortunately for me, they were small, and I just needed to be routinely monitored for growth. This did not prevent me from getting my green card and I was able to return to the United States. This made me realize that you cannot share your dream with everyone because people will not understand what you have received and will always try to discourage you. Most importantly, your dreams will not be realized by just wishing. Colin Powell states that "a dream doesn't become reality through magic; it takes sweat, determination, and hard work."

In 2006, I moved to Berrien Springs, a small town in Michigan, where I had enrolled for my bachelor's in nursing. I was working part-time and going to school full-time. In 2007, I started having issues with heavy periods, back pain, and lots of pressure, so I went to see an OBGYN. The fibroids had grown rapidly, and I needed to have them removed. One of the fibroids was on the wall of my uterus. The result of this would be that I was not allowed to have vaginal delivery, if I ever was to have children. The surgery went well, but two tiny fibroids were left in my Fallopian tube, which would make it harder for me to conceive. I was not thinking about having children at the time, and just told myself that I would worry about them when the time came.

In November 2008, I met Joel, the sweetest guy and the love of my life, and we were married by August 2009. In that same year, I graduated with my bachelor's degree. By January 2011, I was pregnant, and had complications with numerous bleeding episodes and several emergency room visits, as a result. My progesterone levels were low. As a result, I had to be on medication until the end of the first trimester. The bleeding finally stopped, and we were so happy about that. The medication was making me so tired and sleepy that I couldn't study for the exam that I needed to take to get into medical school. And to top it all off, I did end up having a normal C-section delivery.

We were so excited to take Tyivon home. He had a good appetite, was nursing well, and sleeping great from the start. The main issue he had was cradle cap (dry skin on his head). Within a month of him being home, he was prescribed topical steroid creams that we were applying both to his head and face. They worked wonders, at first. We were so excited that everything was clearing up. What we didn't expect was for his face to become much lighter than it was before. At that point though, we didn't care about that, we were just excited that his symptoms were improving. When we stopped, it took a few weeks before he started developing symptoms again, and we'd have to use the cream again. That pattern went on for months.

By the time Tyivon was 6 months old, we had started to introduce food. Of course, he had his favorites, which were mangos and mashed potatoes. He had a good appetite but was not putting on as much weight as his pediatrician would have liked. His weight never dropped below the 50th percentile, however. He always had a runny nose and was breathing "kind of funny" but his pediatrician was not concerned about it. By the time Tyivon turned 12 months, we were ready to leave the cold and the snow and move somewhere warm. Joel and I knew there were three states we were considering with California being our first pick, followed by Texas, and Florida. After a few months and attempts for us to get a job in California without success, we decided to try Texas. I applied to only one job in Dallas and got the job right away. That was it, we were finally going to leave Michigan and were so excited about the move. During my orientation at the hospital, the chaplain told us they were looking for more chaplains. This was exactly what my husband was looking for as well, and he got the job. When you decide to take the first step, God opens the path. Dr. Martin Luther King Jr. beautifully colors this sentiment by stating, "You don't have to see the whole staircase, just take the first step."

Unfortunately, our excitement was short-lived because just a few days after moving to Dallas, we ended up in the emergency room. Tyivon had some wheezing and was coughing. This was the first time we had seen him wheezing and knew something was wrong. At the hospital, they gave him some breathing treatments, and sent us home with some prescriptions, including a rescue inhaler. One night, I woke up because I could hear him audibly wheezing, this time. I turned on the light, and Tyivon was standing up in his crib and breathing very hard. I knew the rescue inhaler would not do it. So, we ended up going back to the emergency room, and this time, Tyivon got admitted.

From that point on, for several years, we were on a rollercoaster. Tyivon had multiple sick visits to his pediatrician and several ER visits. Eventually he was referred to an allergy specialist, and upon testing, found out about his multiple allergies. He started developing skin issues and constipation, as well. Plus, I started noticing that he was very hyperactive, which got me worried even more. The number of medications were just piling up from laxatives, steroid creams, stool softeners, suppositories, rescue inhalers, breathing treatments, allergy medications and so forth. We had to make sure that the meals were safe for him to eat wherever he went. We had an EpiPen, and when travelling, we always took his breathing treatments with us. It got so bad that we had to give Tyivon a suppository pretty much every day. Watching him cry and begging us not to do it was breaking my heart. It got to the point where I could not do it anymore. Tyivon also had frequent colds with fever episodes. He was on numerous antibiotics, ibuprofen and Tylenol. We used to quickly go through many bottles of these medications.

In 2014, I had my daughter, Taliah, via C-section. Unlike her brother, she did not develop any issues, and Tyivon was so excited to have a baby sister. The following year, I obtained my master's degree in nursing, and became a family nurse practitioner. A couple of years later, I went back to school for my doctorate and graduated in 2019 with a Doctor of Nursing practice. By then, a lot of changes had taken place in our family. Tyivon's schoolteacher reported to us that he was not completing his tasks and was very hyperactive. She suggested we have him evaluated by a specialist, which his pediatrician did not agree with, but referred us anyway. During the visit, and without any evaluation, the specialist just recommended putting him on medication for a few weeks. He kept insisting that this was the only way, and I would be very pleased with the difference it would make. He was ready to start right away, and all I needed to do was approve it. Needless to say, we never went back, and never started Tyivon on any medications. Les Brown reminds us, "Don't let other people's opinion of you become your reality." Tyivon's current situation, did not have to be his reality. Sometimes, it is the roadblocks along the way that help us find our purpose. It was time for me to find my own path and make a way where there seemed to be no way. As Ralph Waldo Emerson stated, "Do not go where the path may lead, go instead where there is no path and leave a trail." I was a nurse practitioner who felt powerless, as I did not find my answers in conventional medicine. I kept thinking, "there has to be another way." Therefore, I did the next logical thing and started to do some of my own research.

I started researching through Google and YouTube. I had to use key phrases such as "how to reverse allergies naturally." I stumbled upon

Dr. Josh Axe's channel and watched a video on using essential oils for natural solutions. The information was captivating, and this commenced watching video after video, for hours at a time. The next day, I went to Walmart and purchased essential oils. I started applying them on my son in specific areas, but I did not notice any change, but rather that he started developing small rashes on the application areas, and I stopped. After more research, I found out that not all essential oils are created equal. Some are better than others. But then that confused me, and I started wondering how in the world are people supposed to figure out the quality of essential oils. I had to learn more about essential oils, as they were fascinating to me. That is how I found out that Dr. Axe had a program to train essential oil coaches, so I decided to go through the training and became an essential oil coach. A great Chinese proverb states, "The journey of a thousand miles begins with a single step."

As I was learning about essential oils, I started using essential oils in my family more and more. I started making homemade toothpaste, body butter, dish soap, laundry detergent, and more. I started diffusing essential oils in the house, as well. Then, I noticed a difference with Tyivon, as he was starting to improve. His skin became smooth, his breathing improved, and he was not getting sick as often as before. On top of that, the wheezing episodes went down, too!

As I started digging deeper, I stumbled upon Dr. Natasha Campbell-McBride. She talks about Gut and Physiology Syndrome (GAPS) and establishes the connection between an unhealthy gut and brain and the correlation to chronic physical conditions such as ADHD, depression, eczema, allergies, asthma, autoimmune diseases and so much more. Dr Campbell-McBride established the GAPS diet for healing and treatment. In December 2017, my son started following the GAPS diet and in a matter of days I noticed a huge shift. Even though we did it only for a month, it was mind-blowing. His behavior drastically improved, he was not as picky as before, and his constipation went away. One month went by without Tyivon having any sick episodes, then two months, three months. What a blessing!

I continued my research and found out about functional medicine. I felt as if a big weight had been lifted off my shoulders. For me, it proved that there was a reason why my son had dealt with all these health problems. Provided, if I could find out the root cause, the issues could disappear. It made sense to me to go back to school and study. So, I enrolled in the School of Applied Functional Medicine. I started putting the pieces together. Things started falling into place as I was applying what I was learning within my own family. I learned the importance of a healthy lifestyle, and the fact that there must be balance in all areas of our lives. This includes the food we eat, our movement, proper rest, water, mindset, toxins, our relationships with friends and family, our financial situation, our faith, our jobs, and our activities.

As we were implementing what I was learning, Tyivon was improving, my husband's health issues disappeared, my mother started getting off some medications, and we started losing weight. I told myself that I could not keep it to myself. I had to share it with the world and help other families. I felt a deep sense of fulfillment. As the great Maya Angelou says, "If you are going down a road and don't like what's in front of you **and** look behind you and don't like what you see, get off the road. Create a new path!"

At the end of 2019, I opened a functional medicine coaching business from the comfort of my home. My business aims to help families achieve balance in their lives and find true healing. Several months later, the pandemic started, and I felt called to help. My regular job was put on pause, and I told myself, "Why not?" At a time when so many people were faced with fear, and an uncertain future, I made the decision to go to New York City. In April 2020, I stopped seeing clients in my own practice and went to New York City to work at a local hospital. It was quite an experience to say the least! I was there until things started slowing down. Upon returning to Texas, I continued working with major companies on the pandemic. I still had to travel to other cities in Texas and felt like I was never home. Then, my contract ended at the end of July 2021.

I learned through this experience that you cannot pour from an empty cup. I decided that it was time for me to regain some balance in my life and family and start to focus on building my functional medicine practice. People, more than ever, need help and guidance. I realized that all these weekly travels had really put a stress on me, and my family and it was leading to some health issues. It was time to stop and refocus. In order for me to effectively assist others, I needed to help myself first! As John D. Rockefeller said, "If you want to succeed, you should strike out on new paths, rather than travel the worn paths of accepted success"

I decided to start treating my side hustle as a real business. I desperately wanted to leave my full-time job and I wanted to work from home and have a positive impact on families. I was very excited about the possibilities, and the number of people I could reach out to around the world. I started to educate people through small talks and seminars, both in-person and virtually. I started thinking about opening my own toxin-free skin care line, in order to help other individuals dealing with skin issues or who just simply want clean products. Coming from Cameroon, I had always talked about opening centers back home, but what if I started right here in Texas, and then take it to other countries in Africa? I dreamed of opening centers where people could come and detox, take cooking lessons, coaching sessions, and so much more! Imagine a place where you can find the best of conventional and functional medicine. A place where individuals can come for true healing. The possibilities are endless, and that is exciting.

Now, I would like to leave you with a question. How is your health, and what are you doing about it? I firmly believe that we should unapologetically take charge of our own health, no matter what people tell us. It all starts at home. This is my story and taking back control over the health of my family and myself is the path that brought me to this place. Your path may be completely different, but nonetheless, you can make the decisions leading to the change that you desire. Claim your destiny.

ABOUT DR. MARLENE NANDA ROSANA

Dr. Marlene Rosana is a family nurse practitioner, functional medicine practitioner, essential oil expert, speaker, and best-selling author. She is a dedicated wife and the mother of two beautiful children and is the co-founder and CEO of NewPath Health Institute. NewPath Health Institute is a 100% virtual practice, where she helps entrepreneurial mothers, who struggle with productivity and focus, balance their hormones naturally so they can up-level their lives and successfully scale their business.

Prior to starting to pivot into functional medicine, Dr. Rosana spent over 16 years working in Nursing in long-term care facilities, rehabilitation centers, hospitals, and in patients' homes providing bedside care for the disabled. Last year, she was among the many health care providers who travelled to New York City, which was the epicenter of Covid-19, to assist in providing care at one of the local hospitals.

Dr. Rosana has been featured in Forney Messenger newspaper, has spoken as a guest speaker in churches, and spoken at a Nutrametrix convention both onsite and online streamed nationwide. She has also been featured on the Gaby U Show and on a YouTube channel. She strongly believes that deliciously healthy and balanced living, is key to thriving. Dr. Rosana is on a mission to empower others to achieve balanced living, while crushing their struggles one by one.

newpathwellnesscenter.com | marlene@marlenenandarosana.com | IG: @dr.marlenerosana

Chapter 15

UNCOVERING MY WHY

By Rajinder Rai, PharmD, FAAMFM

"There are no wrong turnings. Only paths we had not known were meant to walk on."
— Guy Gavriel Kay

Do you believe in destiny or fate? I mean, do you really think we are here for a purpose?

If so, why do some people go through so much in their lives and others just cruise by? For an ultra-control freak like me, it's hard to imagine not being in control of every aspect of my life. I had my life meticulously planned, down to each minute of my day, or so I thought. From the outside, I had a picture-perfect life, following all the prescribed protocols. I got my Doctorate of Pharmacy young and was married by age 23. My husband, also a pharmacist, had his dreams of owning his own pharmacy and building his empire, which he achieved. I was content working part-time while being a mom. My life became challenging, though, when my husband had a heart attack, and I was thrust into taking over the operations of the pharmacy. It didn't matter whether I was ready or not, I had to do it. My intention was only to oversee things while my husband recovered, but once I was in charge, I never looked back.

We later went on to buy three more pharmacies and my responsibilities as well as involvement increased. At the time, I was also juggling motherhood, soccer games, piano lessons, PTA meetings, on top of the work. I was literally going one hundred miles an hour but hit a brick wall when I found out I was walking around with three blood clots. I had one in my aorta and two in my lungs. I thought I was just out of shape and kept putting off going to get a check-up. It was at a random dinner with a friend, who happened to be a doctor, when I told her I haven't had a physical in a while. The morning after our dinner, she called me and told me to come in to see her. It was like I had someone watching over me. To this day, she doesn't know what prompted her to call me to come in. All we know now is that I wouldn't be here if she hadn't.

With such a diagnosis, you would think that this would be enough of a wake-up call for anyone to reevaluate their life and reset. However, for me, it was all about the business. I needed to get "fixed" so I could get back to work. I never stopped to ask, "Why did this happen?" I just wanted to get back to my life. I kept saying to myself that "I can't let my patients or my staff down" and that was it. I was literally back to work within 1 week of my surgery. My whole identity revolved around my role as a pharmacist. In fact, I threw myself into even more projects and collaborations in order to create clinical services at the pharmacy. It was like I thrived on the thrill of building more opportunities and relationships.

As our pharmacy business grew, so did the kids. They practically grew up in the back of the pharmacy. They were used to mom having to change plans or abruptly leave to attend to some emergency at one of the pharmacies. Even with pharmacists working for us, I was still directly involved in the day-to-day operations. The "needs" of the pharmacies took center stage in my life, and I allowed myself to get absorbed into that role of constantly putting out the fires. I was on defense 24/7.

Part of running our own pharmacy came with the sacrifice of spending less time with my family. I often missed family events and didn't have free time to visit my parents or extended family. I only celebrated two of my dad's birthdays, in person, over the span of many years, so I was determined to make his 70th birthday special. The plan was to take him on a nice trip. Unfortunately, that day never came. He died shortly after his 69th birthday. My dad had dealt with health problems for most of my life. He had rheumatic fever as a kid and had to have mitral valve replacement, which is an open-heart surgery, at 28 years old. He had one of the very first open-heart surgeries at Stanford back in the 70s. That wasn't the end though as he would later go on to have two more surgeries, as his porcine valve would need to be replaced due to wear and tear, and then finally, he had a mechanical valve placed, which the doctor said would last forever. From the exterior, you would never know that my dad had any health issues. Although he was on multiple medications, I never intervened in his treatment. I assumed the doctor had it all under control. After numerous hospitalizations over the next few years, my dad ended up having his fourth heart surgery. At this point, I just assumed it was going to be routine and didn't think much of it. It was predictable. He would be in the hospital for a week, and then come right back home. Once he was home, my mom would get him back on his feet, just like she always did. I had meticulously chosen a doctor to make sure my dad was scheduled with the best surgeon available. In fact, we waited for the doctor to come back from vacation this time, so he was well-rested and ready to be at his best. I had done everything to assure that this surgery would go as smoothly as possible.

I remember the day of the surgery clearly. My dad was happy to get this over with so he could go back to "feeling good" and my family and I felt the same way. Even the doctor was in good spirits, and was impressed with my dad's will and strength, considering everything that was going on inside his body. Well, despite my best efforts and hopes, it didn't go as planned. There was a complication during the surgery that turned into a 2-month battle for my dad where he was struggling just to stay alive. I put all my faith in God. I knew my faith was strong enough for a miracle. Every time we thought he was taking a turn, his condition turned from bad to worse. It seemed every decision and intervention the doctors made, spiraled him even further downward. He had no advance directive, and we were in no state of mind to give up. At this point he had a trach (a hole in his windpipe to help him breathe), received daily dialysis, and had an open abdominal wound. He had also withered down to just skin and bones. My dad was the one that ultimately decided it was time. On Valentine's Day, just 2 months after the surgery that was supposed to give him his life back, my dad kissed his family goodbye, forever. We were heartbroken.

Once again, I threw myself back into my work. Just a week after my dad's funeral, I was back at work. I needed to just get back to what I did best, work! I decided to work on my Advanced Pharmacist licensure and board certification as a Geriatric Pharmacist. It seemed like the most logical step for both the pharmacy and me. For some reason, about one week before my exam, I just decided I didn't want to go through with it.

A few years later, when my daughter started college, my husband and I suddenly found ourselves as empty nesters. We also began the process of consolidating our pharmacies and reducing the number of locations so it would be more manageable and reduce the overhead. I soon found out I had more time on my hands than I knew what to do with. I was always on the lookout for ways to increase our services while improving the profitability of the pharmacies. It was becoming harder and harder to sustain the pharmacies as reimbursements were drastically going down and costs going up. The bottom line was that I needed to build a financially viable business, so I began to look into billing for clinical services and other ways I could partner with other entities as a consultant.

About three months into my daughter's freshman year at college, she felt a weird sensation after swallowing that alarmed her, so she went to see the health clinic on campus. She was told to get a CT scan. She called me frantically, confused and scared. To reassure her, I had her see her own pediatrician. Although it didn't look like anything more than a swollen lymph node, her pediatrician decided to send her to an ENT specialist. The ENT decided to send her for an ultrasound to take a biopsy of the lymph node. All the tests showed nothing was wrong. The ENT felt that, just to give peace of mind, he would order an MRI of the neck. The MRI raised enough concern that the senior radiologist wanted to do another biopsy from the swollen neck area. Once again, in my thinking at least, all of this was to just give us peace of mind. The results came back with abnormalities, but still without a conclusive diagnosis. At this point, we were still under the impression that we are just doing all of this for peace of mind, not that they were looking for a diagnosis. They sent the sample out to another lab. During this whole process, I hadn't told my daughter about all the back and forth, because I didn't want to alarm her as she was focusing on her upcoming finals.

It was Thanksgiving and we proceeded with plans with friends. Coincidentally, it was my daughter's pediatrician, who is also a good family friend. that was hosting this year. No one knew what was going on other than her pediatrician, my husband and myself. While everyone enjoyed our annual competition of Taboo and Pictionary, the 3 of us were on pins and needles. Our eyes were constantly on my daughter, jumping if she even sneezed. The next day, my daughter began to suspect there was something wrong and insisted we tell her. "It's my body, I should know what's going on!" So, she went to talk to her pediatrician to get her questions answered. After her examination, her pediatrician recommended that we should just go to Children's Hospital instead of waiting for the results. Due to the location of the tumor, and the possibility of it impacting her breathing, she was hospitalized immediately. After that, it was a whirlwind 48 hours going from CT scan to blood tests, to Pet scan, to developing a plan for treatment. There was no time to process all the information being thrown our way. To my complete dismay, I received a call from the doctor saying that the test had revealed some serious concerns that would require treatment to start immediately. Unfortunately, my worst nightmare came true, she had Hodgkin's Lymphoma!

The next day, the oncologist came in to explain the treatment plan. As like most of the other doctors that came to see my daughter, they looked past her, and talked to me directly. As he explained the treatment protocol, my daughter just said, "Why?" We all turned to her as she continued on, saying, "Why did this happen to *me*?" The doctor said, "Well, we don't know *why*, but we have the treatment to take care of this. We have gotten really good at treating this!" His words just weighed on both of us. But at that moment, we just wanted to get the treatment started and over with. On the outside I was calm and composed for my daughter, but internally, I was fighting my own battle consisting of immense guilt and anger. I felt so helpless. I felt like a failure. Somehow, I had failed my daughter. It was the most humbling experience as well. It didn't matter how many certificates I had, how many pharmacies I had, or how financially successful I was. At that moment, I was a mom, just like all the others in the other rooms in that hospital.

For the first time, I was forced out of the responsibilities of our pharmacies. Work would have to wait. They would have to figure it out and function without me. My priority was being with my daughter and getting her through this. Although she was 18, in my eyes, she was still my baby. For the next 6 months my daughter went through her chemotherapy, and I was there with her every step of the way. The whole experience left me thinking about how lucky we were that she was diagnosed so quickly and started treatment in a timely manner. What if she hadn't gone to the campus health clinic? What if the doctor said, let's just wait and see? If this was so overwhelming for me and my family as health care providers, I can just imagine how hard it must be for those with no medical background.

Although she was done with her chemo, and her scans came back clear after her treatment, my journey had just begun. It was like I was underwater, holding my breath, and finally came up gasping for air. The thought of not having an answer for my daughter haunted me, though. The doctor's words echoed in my ears, "We don't know *why,* but we have the treatment..." It made me think about all the patients I must have sounded shallow towards, while giving them a consultation on their medications. I really thought I was a great pharmacist, going over and beyond for my patients. As true as this may have been, I realized that I was doing a disservice by not helping them understand their own "*Why?*".

After realizing how many impactful moments I have lost, being stuck in the pharmacy under my current role, I began to look for opportunities that would allow me to still practice but not be physically in the pharmacy. I began to look into remote patient monitoring, collaborative agreements with doctors, transitional care management, etc., but somehow, I got redirected towards looking into functional medicine. After attending a summit for pharmacists, I learned about functional medicine, and I decided to start learning more. The more I learned about it, the more I realized that uncovering the answer to *why* was actually possible! By staying traditional in a pharmacy, I was enabling the broken system that operates in a bubble, without knowing what other systems of medicine offer. Even under the disguise of medication management, I was not really helping my patients. I was only giving them information about the treatment, not the *why* or the *how*. The amazing part about functional medicine is that it not only looks at the root cause of the presented symptoms, but it also looks at the body as a whole! In fact, it even takes the body, mind, and soul all into account.

Thinking back, I remembered one of the times my dad was in the hospital, and he complained to his doctor, "My stomach doesn't feel right. Can you do something?" I will never forget his doctor's response, "I'm a cardiologist, I don't handle that." This made me ask myself, "How many patients like my dad were left unheard?" Now that I know about functional medicine, I know that gut health is extremely important to whole-body health. Had the doctor looked into his gut health, would he not have had the complications from surgery? Was there possibly a connection? We will never have the real answer, but it is possible things could have been different if the root causes of my dad's symptoms were addressed.

Our current health system is great for "reactive care" meaning it's great when there is an illness, disease, or symptom to treat. When I had blood clots, getting the immediate treatment saved my life, but no one ever looked at *why* it happened in the first place. I was never told what I could do in the future to prevent it, either. I got the attention while under imminent care, but then I was left to figure it out on my own. My dad had chronic conditions but was never taught what to do to improve his condition or reduce his risk for further disease. His symptoms were dealt with as they came up, rather than being proactive. I began to think about all of my own patients and how they started with one condition that oftentimes leads to another, and then the addition of more medications. It was a vicious cycle. I could see it in my life and in the lives of those around me. I truly felt I was doing such an exceptional job making sure my patients were adherent to their prescribed regimen, making sure I had them on a med sync, specialized packaging, customized dosages, etc. Making it as convenient for them to take their medications, was not getting to *why* they were taking their medications in the first place!

To be honest, I think I was conditioned to stay in my own lane. The doctor diagnosed, the doctor prescribed the treatment, and my job as a pharmacist was to educate on the treatment. I never wanted to offend the doctor by questioning them or adding any "extra" information about the treatment that the doctor would not approve of. As I began to work on my certification through the Institute of Functional Medicine, I realized I could do so much more than educate my patients on their medications. I could make a real impact by focusing on educating my patients on preventative lifestyle measures. I was mind blown as to why we were not taught about this in pharmacy school.

As I expanded my knowledge of the principles of functional medicine, it triggered an awakening within myself that I didn't know was there. It was like I had been practicing pharmacy and going through life with a blindfold. I was forced to look at my life from a whole new perspective. Learning to get to the root cause in other people's lives, helped me to identify areas in my own health and life that could use improvement. I was beginning to realize that it was all connected. Once the blindfold was lifted, I was able to see that the universe had been trying to get me to pivot for a long time, I was just too distracted to notice. I automatically gravitated to like-minded individuals and resources that would help me to put all the principles into practice in my own life. One of my favorites is Dr. Mark Hyman, who is on a mission to live to be 120 and wants to live it well. His philosophy is, "What you do today, matters tomorrow." He highly emphasizes a "food as medicine" approach, to which I highly agree with. When I found out diet is the number one cause of preventable disease, I was shocked. I asked myself, "What am I doing filling prescriptions all day, then?" I never talked about nutrition with my patients! I could not understand why this is not part of our curriculum in school. In order to better myself, I joined Dr. Hyman's longevity membership, as I too want to reverse my aging with diet and lifestyle. It's not that I am afraid of getting older, but rather of getting "old." I want to prevent disease where I can, so I can continue to have a vibrant life. This is the same goal I have for my patients. Although, I know there will always be some stress in our lives, how we are able to handle and react to it, is key. I want to help build a community where we are resilient and joyful, literally living our lives to the fullest!

I personally feel that pharmacists are key to helping make this reality. People need support but don't know where to start. Navigating the healthcare system is overwhelming. People often get lost in the system as well. As someone that has been on the other side, and has experienced being a patient, a daughter of a patient and a mother of a patient, I know what it feels like to have the rug pulled from underneath you and to feel lost and confused. The pharmacist is in the right position to help guide patients once they have been diagnosed with a condition. The pharmacist can educate the patient on the current prescribed treatment, but also educate the patient on the alternative lifestyle modifications a patient can do to prevent the condition from progressing or, in some cases, helping reverse the condition altogether. A functionally trained pharmacist can take a deeper dive and help the patient understand the specific system that is out of harmony, rather than just treating the symptoms of a particular disease. A functionally trained pharmacist can bridge the gap between conventional medicine and functional medicine by coming up with a personalized plan that a patient can sustain.

I don't think people intend to be unhealthy, but we live in a world that is bombarded with messages that are confusing and contradicting. We also live fast-paced lives with the illusion we have an abundance of time on our hands. Many have the mindset of "I will do it once..." or "I will quit once..." We make excuses, because it is hard to get out of our comfort zones. Change is hard, but we cannot continue to sit and wait for things to get better on their own. The statistics on chronic diseases are just getting worse and the current reactive health care system is not working. We need to move to a preventive care model. Having the right support is key to achieving this goal, and the support is becoming more widely available. All the authors in this book are helping to start the functional medicine revolution and change the ways pharmacists are able to impact lives. I know functional pharmacists are in a position to empower their patients to take back control of their health and live out their lives to the fullest!

ABOUT DR. RAJINDER RAI

Rajinder Rai, PharmD, is the founder and CEO of *SunRais Health*™. *SunRais Health*™ is a wellness company focused on offering a holistic approach to disease management and lifestyle medicine through a unique digital platform. Dr. Rai has over two decades of experience owning and operating multiple independent pharmacies and creating numerous clinical programs to improve patient outcomes and medication adherence. She is a certified compounding pharmacist specializing in Bioidentical Hormone Replacement Therapy for both men and women.

Dr. Rai holds a certification in Functional Medicine through the Institute of Functional Medicine (IFM) as well as a fellowship through the American Academy of Anti-Aging Medicine. As a strong advocate for the pharmacy field, she is actively involved in the advancement of this industry, and currently serves as the president of the Ventura County Chapter of California Pharmacists Association as well as on the advisory board of PatchRx and GoodRx.

As a highly trained pharmacist and business mentor, Dr. Rai is focused on inspiring young pharmacists as an Adjunct Professor and Preceptor through the University of the Pacific School of Pharmacy. Dr. Rai aims to guide disease prevention from a holistic approach in order to lead others into a long and healthy life.

thrivewithdrrai.com | www.sunraishealth.com | IG: @thrivewithdrrai

Chapter 16

LIGHTING THE PATH TOWARDS HOLISTIC FREEDOM

By Rojan Ghorbannejad,
PharmD Candidate, Class of 2022

"Don't you know yet? It is your light that lights the world."
– Rumi

The narrative, known as "The American Dream," has been spoken about, far and wide. Having grown up in Iran, I often found it impossible to envision this famous dream. While I honor my heritage and feel deeply that Iran has provided me richly with culture, memories, and education, honestly, a huge part of my identity felt incomplete there. As far-fetched as this felt, my goal was to leave my country in order to become the best that I could be.

As an immigrant, I understand the privilege of pursuing my dreams in America. I have worked hard to pave a path for myself while doing everything in my power to become the best that I could be. In this way, I would not only make myself and my family proud but I would also serve as an example for others who share similar aspirations. I want others to know that when they put their best foot forward, no matter what, they can accomplish enormous goals that make a huge impact. Honor, prestige, and success aside, this rewarding path opened at a cost. I left my father, my beloved family and friends, and my home, and this forced a brutal adjustment.

I knew, however, that at my core I had a mission to be someone who would make a positive impact on our world. While these sacrifices were not easy, I fully embraced my passion, attaining a recognized education, and living in an environment where opportunities are plentiful. America offers a great deal to immigrants, but I believe the most enticing aspect of living here is that with the right mind-set, you can become whoever you want. My journey was not linear because I had to start from ground zero. Though there were many sleepless nights, I felt peace in my heart, knowing that I could conquer any challenge and would become everything I am capable of. This way, I could inspire others in similar shoes to do the same. There are central themes throughout my life that have led to my current professional persona. These include the importance of empathy, hard work, physical and mental health, and the will to keep going.

As an empath, I am naturally inclined to feel everything deeply. As a child, and still today, a movie or cartoon can evoke emotions in me quite powerfully. This has infused my love for human connection. I am an avid communicator and a people-person to my core. While this has served me well in my emerging career, as a partner, as a friend, as a daughter, and as an older sister, it may also be quite painful. I have actively put effort into translating these strong emotions into helping people on a deeper level, although there are certainly a million ways to do so. The capacity and desire to connect with others, on a personal level, fueled me to value my empathy, which is the foundation of my decision to pursue my professional goals. All this together has made my long journey worth it.

It took me around ten years to decide what to major in. Immigrants often start out here, taking on jobs that meet their financial needs while they go to school, and this was true for me as well. This heavy weight was central to the start of my professional development. With no mentorship or connections, all I could rely on was my constant ability to ask questions. From contacting counselors to day-long searches on the Internet, I did everything to learn as much as possible about my opportunities. Furthermore, I worked among different settings to gain vast experience across the board.

The most pivotal aspect of my journey so far has been in gaining real life experience. This helped me get much closer to making my decisions, career-wise. As a salesperson, make-up artist, and beauty advisor for three years, I gained many skills: marketing, flexibility, and interpersonal communication. However, the demand of the job to, as my former manager suggested, "fake it until you make it," always rubbed me the wrong way. As a scientist I look for authentic, tangible solutions. Though I did not have the financial freedom to quit immediately, I knew that, eventually, I would have to set my love for beauty products aside, because earning commissions or profit in a hypocritical way went against my vision of empowering people.

Soon after this job, I latched onto another passion of mine: chemistry. I became a tutor at my local community college for four years. Throughout this experience, I realized how fulfilled I felt in sharing my knowledge with others. Moreover, I learned that the best way to fully engage with concepts in chemistry, or any other pursuit, is to mentor other students in personalized ways. These collective experiences helped me get one step closer to understanding how I want to help others.

With the themes of empathy and hard work in mind, I continued to maximize my physical and mental health my goals. I firmly believe that if we are not physically and mentally healthy, our goals are unattainable. This, however, is easier said than done. Throughout my life, I have struggled with a few health issues that have been speed bumps in my path. One of the worst struggles was with depression. As a teenager, I was a perfectionist, which led to crying over an A- in a class. This produced psychosomatic responses such as tachycardia at the mere age of seventeen. This then led me to begin seeking professional help for discomfort, especially during sleep. The symptoms worsened and my parents began to notice its effects as my grades suddenly began to drop and my emotional state worsened.

The first course of action by medical professionals was to prescribe medications, as we all truly believed that they were proven to work in curing or managing health conditions. My psychiatrist put me on an antidepressant. This led to a vicious cycle of reverting to different types of medications. This was a failure, and none of the medications helped me to regain joy in life.

As if the struggles with my depression treatment weren't enough, I was also battling with gut issues from many years prior. Gastrointestinal issues in the form of acid reflux to irregular bowel movements (along with constant headaches) disrupted my daily life from the age of nine. Even with the ingestion of a simple meal, these issues led to feelings of flare-up within my body. As I alluded to above, I am sure you can guess what my doctor recommended for intervention to treat these problems. Yes, indeed it was another generalized medication which only provided a short-term relief from the symptoms.

Now, with everything you have read up to this point about my health issues, let us add Attention-Deficit/Hyperactivity Disorder (ADHD).

From its endless accompanying brain fog to scattered attention throughout the day, everything felt one-hundred times harder. Back in the day, in my hometown, ADHD was painted as a simple and underestimated problem. To others, it was deemed as a condition where you were just "too careless" to sustain concentration, or "too hyper" or "playful" to sit down and finish certain assignments. Little did they know, especially amongst women, this condition had multiple layers. As a student, ADHD conflicted with my high-achieving persona. My mind would just skip an entire question in an exam, or I would write "546" as my answer, instead of the "5,046" that I saw on my calculator. This is just a small fraction of the constant mistakes that exhausted me. I was dealing with this complex issue on top of learning how to perfect English. This all put a huge amount of pressure on my confidence, to the point where I could not perform normally. After that, I decided to seek medical attention.

This was when I took my first college science course in America. My doctor prescribed medication to help with my focus. As people who has always loved quick, efficient solutions, my doctors were my heroes. Taking ADHD medication helped me a lot, and it made me believe that even a small improvement in my symptoms could count as a miracle with medications the only solution.

Constantly thinking about utilizing resources to find the most efficient solution to every problem is how my brain works. As a passionate advocate for human wellness, my initial approach to maximizing people's health was finding the best medication to meet each individual's needs. This desire led me to search for a career in medication expertise. The same way that medical doctors are experts in diagnosing, I desired to become an expert in supporting the individual. Then I started dreaming about inventing a drug that could literally be called, "happy pill."

Right after finishing college, however, I was accepted to Pharmacy school in southern California. Pharmacy school has, undoubtedly, been a challenge. The chemist and health advocate in me, however, was thrilled to learn the different pathways in the pharmaceutical realm. After the first year in graduate school, I decided to apply to be a pharmacy intern. A well-known pharmacy chain hired me as their intern. From their long drive-thru lines and the crowds inside, I felt that their client interactions were rushed, leading to my discomfort. I wanted to spend time with patients to review their medication protocol and regimen, and to answer their concerns. The corporate world waits for no one, though. It was hard to be fair in my interactions with others, ensuring that they grasped all the vital information that I was sharing with them, while staying mindful of the ever-growing lines. This did, however, build my skills in succinct patient communications.

After a year of working within the retail pharmacy setting, I gained enough confidence to apply for a medication therapy management (MTM) internship program. Here, I worked forty-hour weeks for three months during the summer, and MTM gave me that elongated period of time that I needed in order to address each patient's goals and desires.

However, MTM had negative aspects as well. A lot of patients were not receptive to suggestions from pharmacists or interns, as they believed that their medical doctors would help them more. We learned at school that diet and lifestyle have a huge impact on chronic conditions such as Diabetes and Cardiovascular disease.. Most of the targeted MTM patients had chronic diseases. A good portion of them resisted taking their medications, and didn't believe in lifestyle modifications, even when I would suggest them as an easy alternative. There were, however, patients who were much more invested in learning about the effects of lifestyle modifications in order to support their health. These patient interactions inspired me to reflect on other ways that I could expand helping patients more holistically. This breakthrough was beyond exciting.

During my third year of pharmacy school, mixed feelings about my future career began to arise. Add to a global pandemic, and my head began to spin. For three consecutive years my study of pharmacology had me questioning the effects of medication, the duality of its healing powers, and its potentially wretched side effects. As I studied the pathophysiology of diseases, I started realizing that a lot of chronic conditions are preventable, and a lot of health conditions are manageable with the right lifestyle and diet. I thought deeply about how our world needed a wake-up call with the coronavirus, as many just started to take their health and immunity seriously when it came along. My attention started shifting from just focusing on treating diseases and eliminating symptoms to finding out the root cause of them. My mind continued to spin as I thought, "Is there any way that healthcare professionals could prevent illness or even just reduce overall risk in contracting it in the first place?"

In 2020, my entire family contracted the Coronavirus, but my dad was the one who was hit the hardest. Interestingly enough, his lifestyle habits are the least healthy among my family members, as his choices throughout life have led to Type-2 diabetes and liver damage. I did not have the know-how to convince him with science, nor did I have the personal power to persuade him to modify his lifestyle. This led to the ongoing stress and pain I felt, due to my inability to go back to Iran to help take care of him. I lived in true anguish during this time because I was far away from my family and I did not have the privilege to return because of the imposed sanctions imposed by the travel ban - and other limitations I have faced as an Iranian immigrant.

To put it simply, the political conflicts between the Iranian government and the American have made it difficult to travel back to my country of origin. I would do anything to press pause on my financial and family responsibilities here in the U.S. if I could get the first flight back to visit my father. Presently, he has partial lung fibrosis, but thankfully he has been discharged from the hospital. His experience with the virus, plus my own health journey have made me constantly think, "How can we empower our bodies, while supporting and supplementing its natural physiology, to decrease and the chances of getting sick?"

I've tried many different medications throughout the years but, unfortunately, none of them could help me in the way I was hoping they would, which pushed me to search for more tangible, effective, and holistic approaches to care. I would spend hours and hours reading research and articles.

Soon, I was introduced to the concept of functional medicine, and I had a comprehensive food sensitivity test performed on me. I discovered that food inflammation is the exacerbating factor to most of my problems. Then, I started eliminating the inflammable foods from my body, such as dairy and gluten. Only three weeks later, when I went on a vacation where I forgot to take my meds, it wasn't long before I realized that the constant headache, brain fog, and majority of my GI symptoms were gone. With a small change in my diet, I was able to cut down the suffering I've dealt with for many years. This convinced me to trust the power of functional medicine more than ever. Helping people in modifying their lifestyle choices, to optimize their health, became a new passion for me.

Although I still truly believe in the power of medicine, I no longer believe that the traditional approach is the best way to obtain optimal results. By the start of 2021, I began to doubt nearly everything I had believed about western medicine. When it came to my decision to pursue a pharmacy profession, I felt that the community pharmacy setting might not allow me to put in the time and effort that I truly wanted to spend time with my patients so that I could maximize their wellness - to the point that I even started doubting my own profession. I realized that there are better ways to practice medicine, and it does not contradict working against what I'm learning as a pharmacy student. All we need is shifting the focus from obsessing on the symptoms to fixing the root causes.

The world is shifting, and people are starting to realize that there is a better way to practice medicine. This new awareness goes beyond simply seeing medications as the cure-all and should not be the first go-to step.

As the great poet, Rumi says, "As you start to walk on the way, the way appears." My way started to appear as soon as I came across Dr. Christine Manukyan, through LinkedIn. On my quest for answers to all my doubts about my future, she was the light at the end of a very dark tunnel. After we connected, I was honored to earn a scholarship as her very first intern. In March 2021, I experienced a breakthrough, as I entered the world of functional medicine. Since then, I've been offered constant opportunities to learn and grow.

Each person is born with unique talents. I believe we are all here on a mission to maximize those aspects of our humanity. In my opinion, one of our advantages is our ability to embrace all that we have, to live to the fullest. After the ups and downs of my life, I decided to emulate my mentor and serve as the sunlight in other people's lives. On October 1st, 2021, I launched my functional medicine page and I named it *Rojan Wellbeing*™. My parents named me Rojan, which means "luminous day." And, I picked my birthday as my launch date, since it marks a new beginning of my journey. I want to light the way for whoever crosses my path so that I may illuminate the way for them to live their healthiest life. I am committed to educating myself every day about functional medicine, and I will do my best to practice it well.

My passion and love for life runs deep, and I am excited to help others heal and renew their passion and love for life!

ABOUT ROJAN GHORBANNEJAD

Rojan Ghorbannejad is a Doctor of Pharmacy candidate (class of 2022) and a Certified Functional Medicine Specialist™ from *Functional Medicine Business Academy™*. Rojan is the founder and CEO of Rojan Wellbeing. The focus of her practice is helping high-achieving individuals to live up to the full meaning of "well-being" by optimizing their cognitive health.

Prior to opening her functional medicine business, Rojan worked for 4 years at different pharmacies, 3 years as a chemistry tutor, and 2 years as a beauty advisor. After the global pandemic, she decided to expand her knowledge of the holistic approach to mind and body wellness. Through her own health transformation journey with Functional Medicine, she has uncovered the truth about a better way to practice medicine that is more healing than what is currently being practiced in the traditional medicine approach.

Rojan is passionate about illuminating the route for others towards a healthier and happier life. By spending time on one-on-one coaching sessions, ordering Functional Medicine specialized tests in order to find root causes of the problem, and providing personalized lifestyle modification plans, she is taking huge strides forward to help others heal their bodies from within. Rojan has a tremendous love for life and wants to share that not only those within the U.S, but with as many people as she can, all around the world. She is on a mission to help 1 million people heal their mind and body to live their dream life.

www.ROJAN.co | Info@rojan.co | IG: @Rojan_wellbeing

Chapter 17

CHANGING LIVES WITHOUT MEDICATION

By Svetlana Stepanskiy, PharmD

"The best time to fix a roof is when the sun is shining"
– JOHN F. KENNEDY

Today, I feel like I am back in 2001, in a small room of an old airplane hangar, somewhere in Fresno, California. I arrived there with about twenty other people, to experience my first-time skydiving. As I watched instructional videos and the lesson progressed, I realized that my time to jump off the airplane wing was coming closer and closer. In a few minutes I would be 11,000 feet up in the sky, attached to an instructor, and there would be no going back. Even as a young and fearless 19-year-old, I was full of doubts. I was going through such a mix of emotions such as, jitters from the unknown, happiness from new adventure, along with the fear of losing my life. My head was just spinning.

Now, exactly twenty years later, I am going through a very similar, overwhelmingly frightening time of my life. I am drawing direct comparisons with my skydiving experience. This time though, instead of diving with a random instructor, I am with my business coach, Dr.

Christine Manukyan, who is getting me on that airplane, getting me all strapped in and ready to jump. This time, the decision is to become a certified functional medicine practitioner, and it is not a spontaneous decision. I have given it a lot of thought. I weighed all the pros and cons, and I have conducted a lot of my own research.

When I attended pharmacy school, I was taught that there was a medication for every diagnosis or, as people say, there was a "pill for every ill." As I was going through my rotations in the ambulatory care clinic, I was in awe. Every single patient walking into a doctor's office was leaving there with at least one prescription. Antibiotics, antihistamines, pain relievers, antacids, etc. You name it, they've got a drug for it. I could not believe what I saw. Even back then, I understood that this situation was not normal. There should be other treatment options available that are more natural or preventative in nature. I decided to have a conversation with my precepting doctor about this, and all he said was, "That is what patients want, they don't feel that I did my job if I don't prescribe something." His answer bothered me; I could not wrap my mind around it. Patients have an expectation to receive a prescription. I gave it another thought, maybe it is cultural differences that I am not aware of.

I grew up in Latvia, a beautiful small country in the Baltic region of Eastern Europe. I guess this could explain the differences in perspectives, so to an extent, I was able to rationalize it. I was still questioning that type of approach to medical practice, though. Let me be clear, I am not questioning the importance of medication and conventional medicine. Acute problems arise that need immediate attention of a medical doctor, or a visit to an emergency room, require certain medications. We need medication to treat infections, cardiac issues, diabetic emergencies, acute mental health emergencies, and such. What I am questioning, however, is the ability of conventional medicine to actually prevent diseases. Modern medicine is preoccupied with insurance coverage, payments for services, and time management. The more patients you manage to see, the more money you make. Insurance companies normally cover one well check visit a year that usually takes about thirty minutes. How can you possibly have time to discuss with your doctor, and how is your doctor supposed to know who you are, and anything about you, if you only see them once a year for thirty minutes?

When I think of the struggles of many conventional medical providers, I think of my own health issues and my experience dealing with them. A few years ago, I was accidentally diagnosed with Hashimoto's thyroiditis. Hashimoto's is an autoimmune disease that destroys thyroid tissue and causes hypothyroidism. My blood work showed an increase in my TSH levels, and with me being at high risk for developing thyroid cancer, I was referred to an endocrinologist. After more detailed blood work and the discovery of thyroid nodules on ultrasound, my diagnosis was confirmed. Finding out that I had nodules on my thyroid gland made me scared. All I was hoping for at that time was that the nodules were not cancerous. The next step for me was starting thyroid fine needle aspiration biopsy. This is a procedure where a very thin needle is inserted into the nodule within the thyroid gland, in order to obtain cells for the analysis. That was not much fun! But the results came back negative, and I was relieved. At the follow-up appointment, my endocrinologist told me that, based on my bloodwork and ultrasound results, I am still in the very early stages of the disease. She estimated it would be about ten more years until I started experiencing more symptoms of Hashimoto's disease, at which point I would then require medication to relieve my symptoms.

Again, I left the doctor's office with a sense of relief. No cancer, no medication to start, minimal follow up. Easy, right? I can handle that. I have ten more years until I start suffering from fatigue, weight gain, joint pain, heart disease, depression, or muscle weakness, or so I thought. Ten years seemed like a lot. I continued to live my life as I did before the diagnosis. I didn't change my diet, I kept my daily routines as is, I did minimal exercise. Suddenly, I got to the point of my life where I realized that I would require medication, sooner than later. I started having daily tension headaches, which I would bring to the attention of my doctor. I was trying to understand what the cause was. Was it in any way related to Hashimoto's disease? My doctor did not think so and recommended continuing to take ibuprofen. As time went by, and my tension headaches started to grow into migraines more often, I started to get occasional heart palpitations and my extra weight did not go away as easily anymore. Coincidentally, it was time for my annual checkup, and I decided I would discuss the pain I was experiencing during my appointment. I ask about my Hashimoto's again, and again, my doctor did not see any correlation between the headaches and other symptoms. He believed Hashimoto's had nothing to do with my current overall well-being. In addition to that, the lab work that the doctor ordered was all within normal limits. I was advised to continue with ibuprofen, since it seemed to help me manage the pain. I was advised to make another appointment, in case the ibuprofen stops working. Is this the answer I was looking for? No! Absolutely not! I want to know *why* I was having headaches in the first place. I started asking myself, "Why is this happening to me every day? How can I prevent it? If I can't prevent it, then how can I make it better?" I do not want to begin my day with a headache every single morning. As a pharmacist, I know that lifestyle changes can help with all different kinds of ailments, so I began researching if the same applies to Hashimoto's patients. As I explore the wealth of information available online, I find that headaches, in fact, are one of the symptoms of the disease. I read through a list of other symptoms as well, including fatigue, digestive issues, joint pain, heart palpitations, dry skin, and cold intolerance. These were all symptoms I was experiencing, despite having "normal" lab values.

I continued my search for treatment options, and I stumbled upon the functional medicine approach as a way to prevent and treat Hashimoto's disease. The term "functional medicine" was unfamiliar to me. It is not something I've learned before; our professors never even mentioned it or explained a natural approach to treatment. I looked up a definition from *The Institute for Functional Medicine* and found out that "functional medicine model is an individualized, patient-centered, science-based approach that empowers patients and practitioners to work together to address the underlying causes of disease and promote optimal wellness." Basically, it is addressing the root cause of the disease, rather than just treating the individual symptoms. It conveys different aspects of a person's life, from nutritional needs all the way to emotional stressors. The more I read about it, the more I became interested in it.

Going back to Hashimoto's disease, functional medicine helps identify the three main causes: genetics, environment, and gut health. Since I do not recall any family history of thyroid issues in my immediate family, I moved on to researching environmental and gut related reasons. Turns out, Latvia has many environmental problems that can be traced back to the times when the country was part of the Soviet Union. The factories and plants that were built during that time generated high levels of air and water pollution. To this day, many of Latvia's industrial centers operate under former Soviet policies. The Gulf of Riga contains particularly high levels of pollutants due, in part, to the city's poor sewage system. Sulfur dioxide and formaldehyde are often found to be pollutants of Latvian air. I was exposed to all these chemicals throughout my childhood and adolescence and had no control over it. Now that I know about this exposure, I have to do what I can to minimize environmental effects on my body and reduce the toxic burden that comes from outside. I have adopted a low-toxicity lifestyle. I have switched all my skincare and home cleaning products to non-toxic alternatives. I am doing this not just for myself, but I am also making the same change to benefit my entire family. When we put creams and lotions on our skin, or wash our hair, we don't think about the impact it has on our health. The toxins we are exposed to every day have been shown to cause endocrine disruption. This can interact with our thyroid gland due to the fragrance, oxybenzone, parabens, and triclosan with heavy metals being the worst offenders. Our skin absorbs all of these toxic ingredients, and stores them in the tissue within our bodies, causing an immense amount of harm. Surprisingly, the clean skincare I use is not only safe, but I've come to find out that it makes my skin look beautiful and radiant. Now, instead of trying to read all the tiny, hard to pronounce, ingredient names (sodium hydroxymethylglycinate, dimethicone, sodium lauryl sulfate (SLS), polyethylene glycol, retinyl palmitate), on my skincare product labels, I read simple ones. I now see simple ingredients like, aloe vera, jojoba oil, tea tree oil, sweet orange, chamomile, and so on. These ingredients are not only harmless but, in fact, beneficial. Now, my body is absorbing vitamins and minerals through my skin. According to recent labs, my skincare routine is officially helping my body to function at optimal levels. My headaches are nearly gone, and there is no more dryness and irritation on my skin. In some ways, I am also helping the environment because I no longer wash toxins down the drain.

Another aspect worth looking into with Hashimoto's is gut health. According to functional medicine beliefs, disease begins in the gut. The widely used term "leaky gut", also known as intestinal permeability, means that there is damage to the intestinal lining. This damage allows for toxins, bacteria, and other chemical molecules to escape the GI tract and into the blood vessels. Many of the foods we eat are triggers of gut inflammation. Functional medicine offers quite a few dietary solutions that can keep the gut healthy and thus control the symptoms of Hashimoto's disease. The most important would be to eliminate certain trigger foods: gluten, processed foods, refined carbs, refined sugars, and artificial sweeteners. Thankfully, I will not have issues with artificial sweeteners, as I have always excluded foods that contain it. But gluten, bread, pasta, couscous, pancakes, and waffles, this is a challenge. Knowing myself to have previously been unsuccessful in diet changes, I know I would have to start slow. To be successful, I decided to limit the amount of gluten I eat every day, versus completely eliminating it. If I have waffles for breakfast, I will not have pasta for lunch. I look for healthy alternatives, I use more brown rice, quinoa, and buckwheat. Oftentimes, I would skip the side dish altogether and instead opt to have fish and salad for dinner. I increase consumption of gut-healing foods like avocados, bone broth, wild caught salmon, extra virgin olive oil, and fermented foods. Meal planning helps me eat healthier, too. I look for new recipes that would be beneficial for me, before I go shopping. I based my list of what to buy off the recipes I chose for the week. I tried to stay on top of cooking homemade meals, even during a busy work week. Following a healthier diet helps me not only manage the symptoms of Hashimoto's, but also to prevent other chronic conditions such as diabetes, heart disease, or cholesterol.

As I learn more about functional medicine, I recognize that lifestyle changes I make for myself, and my family can also be applied to help others. I started looking into my options, as a pharmacist, to be involved in real health and wellness. My most recent professional experience is in psychiatric pharmacy. I have been working in an inpatient behavioral health facility for over ten years. During my time at the hospital, I have seen a lot of different cases of mental health illness, from anxiety attacks to schizophrenia. Some patients are so severely ill that they never respond to medications and keep coming back. Some patients have never been on medication but end up in the hospital due to postpartum depression or panic attacks. One thing all patients we see have in common is that they leave the hospital on multiple medications. I, as a psychiatric pharmacist, never considered that underlying causes of mental illness can be supported by changing behaviors *without* medication. The changing behaviors discussed by functional psychiatry practitioners are eating an anti-inflammatory diet, supporting gut microbes, optimizing sleep, exercising, treating depression with heat, using bright light therapy, seeking nature exposure, improving social connectivity, engaging in playful activities, and using mind-body therapies. There is proven evidence to support the fact that these treatment methods are successful in helping the brain to heal and process naturally.

Again, I started to ask myself, "How can I get involved? How do I help?" As I was looking for more answers, I stumbled upon a Facebook post by one of my fellow pharmacists. She was asking the group a question about functional medicine. I opened the comments to see an answer from Dr. Christine Manukyan, founder of the *Functional Medicine Business Academy*™. Dr. Christine is a pharmacist who started her own practice, and was inviting others to join her free five-day, *Your Functional Medicine Legacy,* masterclass. The masterclass was specific to us, pharmacists, and how we could incorporate functional medicine into the knowledge we already have, in order to help others. At this point, it was a no-brainer that I needed to join Dr. Christine's coaching academy. One month after joining the Academy, I opened my own practice named *Wholesome You, LLC*™. I have my contracts done and am ready to start helping clients actually heal their bodies. I enrolled in Functional Medicine University, to learn more about clinical aspects and application of putting my knowledge into practice. I followed Christine's advice to not wait until I am "ready to be ready," but instead, to take action now so everything can begin to fall into place.

So today, I can confidently say that I am ready. I am ready to advance my career as a functional medicine specialist. I am ready to educate people about how to take care of their own bodies and live healthier, longer lives. I believe that prescription medication is not the only answer to health issues, there is a natural way to lead a wholesome life. Every person is different, we are individuals, with our own lifestyle, genetics, and environment we live in. I believe that by making functional medicine an integral part of our care, we will drastically improve our quality of life. I see a shift in healthcare where functional medicine plays a bigger role in our imminent future. And I am excited to be a part of this functional medicine revolution.

ABOUT DR. SVETLANA STEPANSKIY

Dr. Svetlana Stepanskiy is a clinical pharmacist, functional medicine practitioner, a health coach, and a mom to three beautiful children. Most recently, Svetlana founded her own virtual practice, Wholesome You, LLC. In her practice, she applies the principles of functional medicine to educate clients about sleep hygiene, anxiety and stress reduction, management of depression and pain.

In 2009, Dr. Svetlana graduated from Temple University School of Pharmacy with a Doctorate of Pharmacy degree. Throughout her career as a pharmacist, Dr. Svetlana has worked in various pharmaceutical settings. She has over a decade of clinical and leadership experience through a community pharmacy, cancer treatment center, acute care facilities, and at a psychiatric hospital. Her experience as a psychiatric pharmacist, is what led Dr. Svetlana to venture out into the functional medicine world in order to help people with mental health disorders to live a healthier life, without medications. Dr. Svetlana has a passion for clean living and advocates for the use of non-toxic skincare and home cleaning products, as she knows the damaging effects these products can have on the human body.

Currently, Dr. Svetlana is attending the *Functional Medicine Business Academy*™ and Functional Medicine University to further advance her knowledge and expertise. As of the fall of 2021, Dr. Svetlana is a Certified Functional Medicine Specialist™ and is working hard to change the lives of her patients through helping them address the root cause of their health issues, instead of just treating the presenting symptom.

www.wholesomeyou.net | info.wholesomeyou@gmail.com | IG: @wholesomeyou_fmp

Chapter 18

SAYING "YES!" TO REWRITING MY STORY

By Tammy Lopez, PharmD, BC-ADM, CDCES

"At any given moment, you have the power to say this is not how the story is going to end."
— UNKNOWN

Life has not always been easy for me and after going through many challenges, I finally made decisions to change the course of my life and reclaim my health, both mental and physical. I would like to start the story with what life events led up to me developing severe gut and other health issues, and how I was able to overcome them with functional medicine.

After living with severe acid reflux for 8 months, taking the maximum dosage of pantoprazole (a proton pump inhibitor), Pepcid, Tums, and lidocaine solution every 4 hours at night just to sleep, I knew this was not the way I wanted to live my life. I had many responsibilities at the time including being a single mom of a young child, working full time as a Pharmacy Manager and a Clinical Pharmacist, and I honestly could not afford to be unhealthy. I knew I needed to regain my health and get my life back for me and for my son.

I met my fiancé when I was an undergraduate in college in my early 20's at a family wedding. We talked off and on for years after at different family events since we had mutual family through marriage. When I finally graduated pharmacy school, we ran into each other again after about 6 years from first meeting and decided to start a relationship. We lived about an hour away from each other, so I decided to move to the city he was living in, so we didn't have to drive back and forth to see each other. About 6 months into the relationship, we unexpectedly got pregnant, but had a miscarriage. We weren't quite ready for children at that point, so we didn't try again until years later. After about 10 years of being together, we tried to conceive again, but had another miscarriage. This made me feel regretful that we waited so long to try again, as I was in my late 30's and didn't feel like I had much time to have the two children that I always wanted. I spent time concentrating on my career, but at this point I was ready and longing to be a mother. We tried over the next year to get pregnant before the doctor said we would look into any testing, and after countless prayers and right about the year mark, we were pregnant with our miracle baby.

I was about 6 months pregnant when I arrived at work and noticed that my hands were so swollen, they had turned into sausages. I panicked and took my blood pressure while in my clinic office and recall it to be in the 160s/high 90s, which is abnormally high. I went to the hospital triage where they could monitor my blood pressure levels as well as the baby. While there, I was put into a room where they turned off the lights to calm me down and put on an automatic blood pressure monitor that checked my vitals every 5 minutes.

While lying there, I glanced over at the most recent level, and it read around 200/120, which was the highest blood pressure that I'd ever seen! I quickly hit the nurse's button as no one was coming in to check on me and no alarm was going off. I told the nurse that they needed to give me something immediately to lower my blood pressure before I have a stroke right then and there. I did not want to die, and I did not want anything to happen to my unborn child! It was truly one of the scariest moments of my life! To think that I literally could stroke out and possibly lose my baby, was terrifying. I kept thinking, "I didn't make it this far just to have something go wrong." The nurse finally gave me medication to lower my blood pressure and as a result, my pregnancy was determined to be high-risk. That day, I was diagnosed with pregnancy-induced hypertension.

At that point, I was put on limited physical activity and then bed rest in the hospital. I was told I was going to be on bed rest for 6 weeks, and after only 8 days in the hospital, my son's heart rate was dropping. I remember the nurse walking into my room saying, "How about a birthday today?"

I didn't quite comprehend what she was saying, so I said, "What do you mean?"

She said I was going to deliver in an hour, due to my baby's heart rate dropping. I did everything I could to not have a panic attack. My family lived an hour away, so I immediately called everyone I could.

While everyone was rushing to get to the hospital, I took deep breaths, prayed, and tried to get in a Zen mode in order to make it through the next few hours. My son was delivered via emergency C-section at 28 weeks and 6 days weighing in at only 2 pounds 7 ounces. His lungs were not fully developed, he needed to be on a CPAP machine, and he needed two platelet transfusions. It was clear that he needed to stay in the NICU for the remainder of his gestation period to grow, which turned out to be 11 weeks. It was so hard to leave my baby and not be able to bring my child home after having just given birth to him. It didn't fit into the expectation of what I *thought* was going to happen when I had my baby.

I was at the hospital for hours a day, keeping in touch with the staff about his health and oxygen levels. He was doing well for the most part. That is, until the nurses accidentally overdosed my son by administering five times his normal dose of Aldactazide, a diuretic medication used to drain fluid from his lungs. Being a pharmacist and understanding that mistakes can happen, there were three people that checked my son's dose prior to administering it and somehow that mistake still happened! I was livid, angry, and scared. The provider assured me that my son would not have any residual effects, and that his labs were stated to be normal. I kept thinking, "How do you know that he won't?" My mental and physical stress levels were pretty high considering the concern of the effects of my son being born prematurely and everything he has gone through, all while healing from my C-section.

With only having FMLA for 8 weeks, and my son being in the NICU for 11 weeks, I worked part-time from home to extend my time to be with him. I needed to be with him every day in the hospital. The day he came home, I was ecstatic! I finally had my family, all together, at home. The sad part was that I had to return to work, full-time, the very next week. This news crushed my heart as I felt like I had no real time to spend with my newborn son, and I had no other option. As the breadwinner of the family, I also carried the medical insurance, so I did not have the ability to work part-time. My pharmacy job required 40 hours in order to keep my position and benefits. As much as I longed to be home with my son, I was the one that held everything together, for our family, financially.

As we transitioned to having our son at home, a full night's sleep was a thing of the past. I was a zombie for a while and wasn't sure how I made it through the day at work. I didn't even have time to just get used to my son being home, much less while working 40 hours a week, at 10-hour shifts. I had never been that sleep-deprived before, and now understood what I heard other parents talk about. I was so tired that it literally hurt.

Despite the lack of sleep, there is nothing like the love you have for your child. I cherished all his little noises, facial expressions, and silliness. As we became used to our new normal at home, I started to notice some different changes in my fiancé fairly soon after my son arrived home. Without going into any specifics, he just started to slowly check out of our relationship. There was no communication about what was going on with him, and no explanation as to what we could do to work on it. No matter how many times I tried to save our relationship, it just wasn't working. I didn't understand how we had just gone through so much with trying to have a child, going through a high-risk pregnancy, and living through three months in the NICU with our new-born son and still, it wasn't working.

For months, I went back and forth about whether I should leave the relationship because it brought me so much guilt to think my son would not have both of his parents to raise him in the same home, and he was so young. Despite all my best efforts, I couldn't carry this relationship alone. The stress from the relationship was starting to affect my health, and my blood pressure was beginning to consistently rise again. I felt that if I stayed, it would literally kill me because it had such a negative effect on my mental and physical health and my son needed me.

One day, I was driving home from work and for the first time in my entire life, I audibly heard a voice in my head telling me, "Now!" And I understood that it meant to get out now. It took me a second to realize what was going on, but as much as I prayed for an answer as to what I should do, I knew that this voice was my sign that I had to leave the relationship, now. I never doubted what that voice was telling me. And after twelve and a half years together, I made the decision to tell my fiancé he had to leave. All he said in response was, "Okay." He left without batting an eye or saying anything else to me. No fight for our family, no explanation for anything, nothing. I felt so let down, and my hopes for our family went out the door. I knew that if God wanted me out of that relationship, it would be because He had something better for me and my son.

My son was 18 months old at the time of our separation. I now had to find a new way of life with managing work, 10-hour shifts, and leaving my child in daycare for 11 hours a day, while also adjusting to home life, by myself, with none of my family living in my same city. That sudden transition was highly stressful. I had to change my mindset and I started saying to myself, "It's sink or swim time! I've been in stressful situations before, and I can do this!"

A few months after my separation, we couldn't agree on a shared custody agreement, so we ended up going to court. After about 8 months, and tens of thousands of dollars, I obtained majority custody. However, now my son would get more overnights with his dad than he previously had. On the nights that my son was with his dad, I literally almost had a panic attack. To me, it wasn't natural to be away from my young child. I had not slept for more than 4 to 5 broken up hours a night, and sometimes only 2 hours when my child was with his father. I then had to get up the next day to work another 10-hour shift. I felt robotic at work at times and just went through the motions of my responsibilities. I was a zombie for a while. Living with high stress for the previous few years, I knew that my body could not handle the lack of sleep and high stress, and eventually it caught up to me. I developed severe acid reflux and gut issues on top of my insomnia and high blood pressure.

For eight months, I was sleeping upright in my bed every night just so my esophagus would not feel like it was on fire. My gastroenterologist put me on the maximum dosage of the acid reducers pantoprazole and Pepcid, and I took tums throughout the day. It helped me, but not 100%. I started having more pain at night despite being on these medications and was also given Lidocaine solution to numb my esophagus. It only lasted about 4 hours until I had to get up again to take more. I was so fed up with being in chronic pain, enduring high stress, and not being able to sleep, that I started to look for any alternative that would help me. I was frustrated that, as a pharmacist, with the knowledge of all the medications and what should have helped, I was out of medication options. I developed vitamin B12 deficiency from the acid reducer medications, which lead to neuropathy causing numbness and pain in my fingers and hands, despite taking a vitamin B complex daily.

This was my breaking point. I was looking for any remedy or option that would help me because prescription medications were not. So, I immediately started doing research, trying different natural alternatives like aloe vera juice and deglycerized licorice. They didn't work, and the latter supplement negatively affected my blood pressure. I kept thinking, "I have a young child that I must take care of" and I knew I could not continue living in pain and not sleeping. Living this way was going to cut my life short.

I started making lifestyle changes like cutting out caffeine, coffee, spicy foods, tomatoes, and chocolate. But it seemed like everything I ate was making my stomach hurt, even when I was not eating. In my research, I stumbled upon the term "functional medicine" and found YouTube videos of functional medicine providers offering natural remedy information. I had never heard of the term before, and it intrigued me. I had heard of Naturopathic Doctors, but not Functional Medicine Practitioners. As I was looking for a local practitioner that could possibly help me, I typed in functional medicine on Facebook and found a pharmacist group called the Functional Medicine Pharmacists. I saw that there were other pharmacists that were also practicing or learning more natural alternatives to health. In pharmacy school, they touched on vitamin supplements, but little on herbals or nutraceuticals (food that has proven medical benefits). This was a new area for me, but I was willing to learn. If it helped heal me, and I could get my life back, I would do it. I was willing to try anything.

On the Facebook group, pharmacists posted questions asking for guidance on treating patients with functional medicine, or questions for themselves. One pharmacist stated they were dealing with acid reflux and asked for alternative recommendations from prescription medications. I was looking at the responses, and one of the pharmacists asked the author of the post if they had heard of the "Gut Protocol." I was eager to learn what this protocol was all about, so I asked if I could get more information as well. The pharmacist messaged me and stated that she was selling a natural combination product that helped her with her own personal gut issues. The product balanced the gut-brain-axis, which I was soon going to learn more about. I did my research and figured, what do I have to lose?

I learned that the connection between the brain, gut, and microbiome (bacteria in the gut) have a huge influence on overall health. It impacts digestive issues, such as irritable bowel syndrome, and also mental health conditions like depression and anxiety. Therefore, whatever is happening in our gut, can directly affect our brain function and behavior. Learning this gave me a newfound hope that something could help me with my health issues.

I started the pre/probiotic and herbal supplements that the other pharmacist recommended. This directly addressed all the areas needed to balance the gut-brain axis. I had an endoscopy scheduled 1.5 months after I started it and figured I would give the product until then to see if it improved my symptoms. Within the first week, I was able to have a good night's sleep. I also noticed my mood was significantly improving and I didn't lose my patience as easily. My stomach had less pain, so I was able to lessen the pantoprazole and Pepcid from twice daily to once daily. I started to notice I was only getting pain when I took the prescription medications, so I was beginning to wonder if I still even needed them.

By the time of my endoscopy, I thought, "What if my insides are full of ulcers?" I had never been put under before, so I was nervous on several levels. Once the doctor was done, she said everything was normal in my gastrointestinal tract. "Seriously?", I thought to myself. "What the heck could be causing me so much pain if nothing was there?" The gastroenterologist recommended I continue with my high dose medications twice a day, as it seemed it was working. In my mind, I said, "Hell no!" I was tired of the side effects, and the product I was taking seemed to be healing my gut and making me feel better. So, I stopped my prescription medications cold turkey after I got the news from the endoscopy test and haven't had the return of my acid reflux ever since. I was able to heal my gut naturally, instead of masking my issues and just suppressing my stomach acid with the prescription medications. I felt like I finally had my life back!

This situation totally changed my perception of prescriptions and the role of functional medicine. I thought to myself, "Why do more people not know about this?" This lit a passion inside my soul of how I could help people who were in my same situation to get better, naturally, without all the side effects of traditional medication. It's like I found my purpose! It changed my whole mentality of prescription medications and medication guidelines. Why are nutraceuticals and functional medicine practices not the first line in all our guidelines? The majority of my patients at the pharmacy are on acid reducers, antidepressants, and sleep aids. I felt like I had to tell the world about my new insight and discovery!

Around the time I began researching functional medicine, I met a fellow woman pharmacist, Dr. Christine Manukyan. Dr. Christine was starting her business coaching group, called the *Functional Medicine Business Academy*™. She was looking for other women in the pharmacist community who were interested in starting their own virtual functional medicine business. Once I thought for a moment that I could have my own business, and have more time with my son, I felt like God had dropped this opportunity in my lap! I made an appointment to discuss her program, and it was like this woman was speaking straight to my soul. I got full-body chills! I signed up and we started our business coaching group on November 11th, 2020. We learned how to start our LLC or S Corp, set up specialty lab and nutraceutical wholesaler contracts, layout our websites, how to promote our business, amongst many other skills. I learned of many factors that could be the root cause of various health conditions like environmental toxicities, food allergies, gut health, and imbalanced hormones. When these are tested and directly addressed, medications may not need to be used and health can be fully restored. When you treat the root cause of the symptom, you're actually *healing* the body. I feel like this is where healthcare should be going and should have been all along.

Since starting my own LLC, I've furthered my education on how I can best understand and help my patients as a whole, because there are so many facets of conditions and symptoms that clients will present me with. Realizing that patients utilize numerous prescription medications for their health, I have obtained a certification in Pharmacogenomics, in order to see how a person's DNA could affect the way they are responding to medications or if that could be contributing to bad reactions and side effects causing ill health. I can also find which medication is best for them using precision medicine, if needed. I've also completed my certification as an Integrative Pharmacist Specialist and am currently working on my Functional Medicine Practitioner Certification. In addition to these certifications, I am a Board-Certified Advanced Diabetes Specialist and Certified Diabetes Care Educator and have been working with patients with Type 1 and Type 2 diabetes for over 15 years. Diabetes will be a big focus in my practice because I have the tools to directly help my patients gain control over their blood sugar and potentially find what is actually causing the blood sugar impairment in the first place.

With the understanding that prescription medications and functional medicine certainly play a role in health, I feel mindfulness and spiritual aspects of our lives need to be addressed as well. I've been working with another pharmacist coach, Dr. Christina Fontana. She helps women focus on rapid transformation and releasing subconscious blocks, which has helped me to heal a lot of my past wounds, practice mindfulness, meditation, and learn how to energetically balance myself. The mind-body connection plays a huge role in healing disease, and I saw that in my own healing journey. Our beliefs, thoughts, and emotions directly impact our state of health. As I've gone through my transformation journey, Dr. Christina has helped me release many of those blocks that kept me stuck in my life and health. She uses hypnotherapy, quantum physics, spirituality, and intuitive coaching, so I can step into my highest self as I learn to incorporate and teach these skills when working with my clients, too!

With the certifications, coaching, previous years of clinical experience, in addition to my personal life and health experiences, I believe this has prepared me for this chapter of my life. I am now able to shape my unique client services and design my own business that will bring healthcare to my clients, at a whole other level. With education and having the ability to order specialty labs, genetic testing, and use diet and medical grade nutraceuticals if needed, I can help my client's physical body. I also have the tools, experience, and resources to help at a deeper level by looking at the spiritual and mental aspects of what could be contributing to symptoms, pain, and diseases. I can help the client in so many different realms. My direct focus is on helping clients regain their health and heal from diabetes, gut issues, and mental health challenges. I also have a desire to help single moms to build their stress resiliency. I believe that taking the approach to focus on mental wellness is truly the cause of the majority of our world's health crisis, and I will help one person at a time.

My aspiration since I had my son was to be able to work part-time at my pharmacy job to have more time with him and not miss those precious milestone moments. I am now working part-time at my pharmacy job, and my son loves that I am home more. I have also started my new adventure in becoming a female entrepreneur through owning my own Functional Medicine Practice. I truly feel like I found my purpose in helping others to change their lives. Yes, I have been practicing as a traditional pharmacist for about 18 years, but let me tell you, it's never too late to change your story. If I can do it, I know you can too!

ABOUT DR. TAMMY LOPEZ

Dr. Tammy Lopez is a Certified Functional Medicine Specialist™ from Functional Medicine Business Academy™, Integrative Medicine Practitioner, and clinical pharmacist. Dr. Tammy is board certified in Advanced Diabetes Management and certified in Cardiovascular Disease Risk Management, Medication Therapy Management, insulin pump and continuous glucose monitoring, Pharmacogenomics, and is a Certified Diabetes Care and Education Specialist. She is the founder and CEO of *Life Engagement Achieves Purpose*™ (LEAP). She helps people with diabetes, gut issues, and mental wellness challenges aiming to discover the root cause of health issues, reduce or discontinue medications, and empower her patients to take their life back and attain their highest potential.

Dr. Tammy has been in healthcare for 18 years as a retail and clinical pharmacist, holding numerous leadership roles over the years. 16 of those years, she has been the pharmacy manager and clinic coordinator, overseeing and managing patients in both diabetes and cardiovascular disease management programs, in a community pharmacy setting. She has worked with patients with pre-diabetes, Type 1 and Type 2 diabetes, hypertension, and high cholesterol. Initially, Dr. Tammy started in diabetes care through a national study sponsored by GlaxoSmithKline through the American Pharmacist Association called the "Diabetes Ten City Challenge". At this challenge, she was the pharmacist site coordinator and clinical pharmacist for her city that participated in the study. Out of 10 cities in the study, Dr. Tammy's site was named top 3 for cost savings to the employer and overall patient outcomes. Over the course of the study, Dr. Tammy has participated in numerous publications, including on the radio and in the news, regarding the progress of her study site. At the end of the study, she continued to build on the program and worked with over 100 patients annually.

This challenge eventually led her to start a cardiovascular program with similar successful results. She has now helped numerous patients discontinue or significantly reduce their medications through changing their diet, medication management, and developing healthy lifestyle habits and incorporating physical activity. Through her ongoing leadership in the diabetes program, she was able to publish the results of her continued success of patient outcomes in the *Innovations in Pharmacy Journal*.

Dr. Tammy was recently invited to share her expertise and experience on a panel with the President of the American Pharmacist Association. This unique experience was a public discussion regarding implications of COVID-19 on patients with diabetes, access to care, vaccine eligibility, and lifestyle. Dr. Tammy has seen how stress and mental health challenges play a big role in affecting overall wellbeing, sometimes resulting in a diabetes diagnosis. She has found that gut problems (otherwise known as "leaky gut") are often contributing factors to chronic disease conditions, mental illness, chronic inflammation, and uncontrolled diabetes.

Dr. Tammy's mission is to help people suffering from diabetes, gut issues, and mental illness, find the root cause of their health issues, through functional medicine and specialized lab testing. She helps patients find natural alternatives to manage their health and reduce or discontinue medication, if possible. Dr. Tammy empowers her patients to take a courageous LEAP™ toward health and regain their quality of life.

drtammylopez.com | drtammylopez@gmail.com | IG: @dr.tammylopez

Chapter 19

FROM DARKNESS INTO THE LIGHT

By Zsuzsanna Coniglio, PharmD

"There is a place that you are able to fill, that no one else can fill. Something you are to do, which no one else can do."

— FLORENCE SCOVEL SHINN

My journey of enlightenment began in the summer of 2015. To the outside world, I might have seemed like a successful, decently well-off person with a great job, loving family, beautiful home, and occasional nice vacations. This was probably because I am not a person to share my real struggles on social media. However, deep inside, I felt lost, unmotivated, living in a rut. Life primarily consisted of eating, working, and sleeping. I lost sight of all things I should be grateful for. Lying in bed at night, I'd often reflect back on the day with disappointment. I just had no idea yet of how powerful my own thoughts could be.

Growing up in Romania, I always ate healthy, home cooked meals with tons of veggies and fruits. I stayed active doing ballet and gymnastics in elementary and middle school, then taking up dance lessons at the local youth club, not to mention the daily 10-story staircase I had to go up in order to get inside our home. Let's just say, I was not a fan of our elevator, and getting stuck in it was my nightmare. Moving to the United States, and having my daughter at 16, made me more determined than ever to stay in shape and create the best life for her. Three months later, I was back in shape and feeling great about our future. Having her made me grow up faster, make smarter decisions, and keep my focus on becoming a pediatrician. Fast-forward four years, it was time for college. I decided to attend the local community college for the first two years of pre-med, while working full time at a great local restaurant, where I eventually met my future husband. We soon started living together and making plans for our future. He always supported my dreams of becoming a doctor, and we started planning to expand our family and buy a home. That summer, we found out I was pregnant with our son and bought a beautiful three-bedroom apartment. We were excited about this new chapter in our lives! My pregnancy was great, however, I gained significantly more with this pregnancy than my first. I wasn't too worried at all about the weight gain, as I had a strong workout routine before pregnancy, and fairly healthy eating habits.

Delivery day arrived, and we were so excited to meet our little one. Our excitement soon was shattered as he was born, and doctors and nurses were trying to figure out what was wrong with him. We couldn't tell just yet what the worry was about as he was all wrapped up in a blanket when they let me hold him for that brief moment, right after he was born. I just knew, he had to be ok. They rushed him up to NICU, and a bit later they asked if we wanted to go see him. "Of course!" we said. Seeing him in that incubator was a sweet moment of tranquility. I pulled the string on a toy bunny that sings and used to play it for him when he was in my belly. To the sound of the music and my voice, he turned his sweet little face towards me, our eyes met, and my heart melted in an instant. He is my little boy, and I just knew we must do anything and everything for him to have a normal life. The next day we learned he has something called APERT syndrome. Its main characteristics include prematurely fused sutures in the skull as well as fused fingers and toes, all of which will require several surgeries to make space for the brain to grow and allow functionality of the extremities. Some cases are more severe than others, and there may or may not be some developmental delays as well. We were hoping, praying, and leading with faith and the belief that he will grow up to be an amazing human being. I am beyond grateful that God chose me as his mother, listened to our prayers, and that we have been able to witness his amazing journey and transformation from birth. He has turned into a healthy, happy and thriving young adult. He has amazed us over the years with his amazing loving character, his intelligence, creative side (drawing 4 huge self-portraits in his high school art class and other artwork chosen to be displayed), and grit. In his senior year in high school, he became the student manager of his high school's basketball team, and he was also chosen as prom king. Then, he went on to university where he sought out the basketball coach, scheduled an interview, and landed the student manager position at the university, all on his own. A year later, because of the pandemic and closing of the university, he sought out and secured, once again, the student manager position for the basketball team at the new university. He is my role model. He is a great example to me as to what having a great self-esteem and belief in yourself, can accomplish.

After finishing my first two years at the community college, I went on to continue my pre-med at the local university. Already having two young kids, seeing and experiencing the pressure all pre-med students go through, and putting in excessive volunteer hours, I started questioning if this is what I really wanted. I met and befriended a wonderful girl in undergrad, who went on to pharmacy school, and she helped persuade me to follow in her footsteps. She shared her experience of what she was learning in pharmacy school and explained how pharmacy relates to medicine. She explained that I could have more freedom to work the hours I wanted, plus, could finish up my degree sooner, without the need for residency. Within 3 to 4 months of deciding on the pharmacy career, I aced my PCAT, and was accepted into pharmacy school. As faith would have it, the first day of pharmacy school, I met and befriended the most amazing and inspirational "Wonder Woman," Dr. Christine Manukyan, who is one of my best friends to this day. This woman is the reason why I am sitting here today writing this book. She is also the inspiration for so many of my other choices, that led me towards stepping out of the darkness, and into the light.

The four years of pharmacy school went by in a flash. I enjoyed learning about the body, the medicines, their mechanism of action, and seeing how it all ties together. Graduating with high honors as a Doctor of Pharmacy, was a special moment to experience. My husband, our two children, grandmas, and my brother were there to commemorate this special milestone. The future seemed bright. At this moment, more than ever, I got to look back with great appreciation for all the love and support I had from my husband and both grandmas, who helped me out so much and made it possible for this to happen. From full days and late-night babysitting, to helping out with the housework, I truly need to give credit where credit is due. I am not sure I would have been able to go through the demanding curriculum of pharmacy school if it wasn't for this unwavering, reliable support from my immediate family. Halfway through pharmacy school, we decided to sell our apartment to help with balancing our finances until after graduation, as the demands of pharmacy school and 2 kids did not allow me any time for work, and we still wanted our kids to have a great childhood and experience fun adventures growing up.

Life then commenced as a full-time, working mom, of two kids. Not one to be shy of hard work, I threw myself into my new profession 110%. This never went unnoticed and a few months later, I was offered the manager position at a pharmacy close to home, which I could not refuse. I started earning a good, stable income, and making a greater financial contribution to our household. However, this new income also came with a hefty 30-year student loan, for which the monthly payment was more than my rent for our one-bedroom apartment we had just a few years before. It was also time to invest once again into our own property. This time we decided to purchase a home. Soon enough, we found our dream home and bought it. This new mortgage, along with the student loans, and other household expenses, ate away a good chunk of my new salary every month and kept me working tirelessly over the years. One year turned into 5, then into 10, and before I knew it, I was grinding away at work, working hard as ever just to make ends meet. On top of it all, I felt the burn-out that so many others have mentioned. I was too tired to take care of my own health, to work out or eat healthy.

My struggle with achieving and maintaining a healthy weight started shortly after giving birth to my son. With so much weight to lose, a new baby to care for, my daughter starting elementary school, and myself in undergrad studying full time, I realized it wasn't going to be as easy to lose the weight this time around, as I had previously thought. When my son was around 6 months old, I started with Jenny Craig, then over the years I tried numerous other diet fads such as Nutrisystem, Atkins, Fruta Planta, Herbalife and HCG injections just to name a few. Most of these diets yielded small changes of weight loss and were short-lived. Each time I gained the weight back, I'd feel defeated and disappointed and on the lookout for the next miracle weight loss trend. As the summer was approaching in 2015, I felt I had enough of short-lived, unhealthy diet trends. I promised myself I would not go on any other fad diet. Instead, I'd search for a healthy way to lose the weight and keep it off. This new "diet" had to be something that could be easily implemented into my busy lifestyle. It just happened that the Universe threw me a sign. One day, as I was browsing through Facebook, I stopped and paused in awe at my "wonder woman" bestie's post about her amazing physical transformation. I reached out to her right away to see what her secret weapon was. I was expecting to hear something familiar, and when she started to tell me about healthy protein shakes, I started shutting down as I've tried protein shakes before and it didn't work for me. This time, however, I kept an open mind and she proceeded to explain the entire system. She explained how it all works together and the health benefits were tangible. It was the first time ever that I've heard of alkalinity and intermittent fasting. Skeptically, I decided to give this new system a try, and after much research of my own, I joined this health and wellness company for its amazing products that provided the results I was looking for. I had a plan that helped with the healthy nutrition that could easily be incorporated into my busy life.

Joining this company and the amazing community proved to be the springboard to my own health and wellness journey and paved the way to my newfound passion for nutritional rebalancing, functional medicine and personal development. I was able to lose the weight the healthy way and maintain it for years to come. I finally felt better and more energized than I had for years. For the first time in years, it felt like I had clarity, I had a purpose, I had a vision for the future. I dug into self-development and would listen to everything from Tony Robbins, Jim Rohn and people alike. I'd also listen to audiobooks such as, *As a Man Thinketh* by James

Allen, *Think and Grow Rich* by Napoleon Hill, *How to Win Friends and Influence People* by Dale Carnegie, *The Power is Within You* by Louise L. Hay, and *The Power of the Spoken Word* and *Your Word is Your Wand* by Florence Scovel Shinn. Any and all of these I highly recommend for everyone to read or listen to. I can honestly say, these books had a great positive impact on my life, my perspective and my mindset overall. Before I was just going through the motions, ebbs and flows of daily life, and now, I am more mindfully aware of my thoughts and how they shape my reality. I catch myself when negative thoughts spring up and try to bash them away and not allow them to linger on for long periods of time, like I have in the past. This in itself has been a huge relief in my mindset. My favorite quote from Florence Scovel Shinn is this one I quoted in the beginning of this chapter. She also gives many great affirmations for all types of situations. One of my favorite affirmations she also taught me is, "I give thanks for my permanent happiness, my permanent health, my permanent wealth, my permanent love." I speak this over myself, often.

While I'm on the topic of self-development, I have to tell you about my amazing experience at my very first Unleash the Power Within (UPW) event hosted by Tony Robbins I attended, virtually, in March 2021. The entire event was amazing, but what really captivated me and gave me that "aha" moment was on the last day of the event when Master Co talked about energy healing. During a demonstration, he asked us to do a few movements with our hands, then with our palms facing up. He started circling with his finger as if it was above our palms. I truly felt the energy, from miles and miles away, circling above my palm. I felt the pause, and then as he reversed the circle in the opposite direction. This was a pivotal moment that led me to research and sign up for a course, in order to learn more about Reiki (Universal Life Force Energy). I am excited to dive into this, new to me, dimension of healing and wellness.

Interestingly enough, one of the most significant revelations along this journey was the realization of just how little, as health care practitioners, we were taught about preventative medicine, such as nutrition, herbal supplements, and the importance of a healthy mind, body, and soul, meditation. This along with other practices that may help prevent, and maybe even treat, some of the common diseases we see on a daily basis was so enlightening. At the very least, these could be great complimentary additions to a patient's current treatment regimen, resulting in a greater number of favorable outcomes. I understand for some patients, it seems simpler to just swallow a pill and go on with their life. That's why it's important to educate them on the importance of addressing the underlying issue that led to the disease itself, in the first place. This can give the patient some sense of control over their health and encourage them to be more proactive in their treatment.

Over these past few years, I've become extremely passionate about nutritional rebalancing. I was shocked to learn just how bankrupt and void of nutrients our vegetables and fruits are today, as compared to 50 years ago. This is mostly due to over-farming and the wide use of pesticides. If we are to keep our body in the best health possible, we need to eat even more vegetables and fruits to make up for the lost nutritional value, or at a minimum, supplement our diets with a high-quality vitamin and mineral formula. Our bodies are starving for these nutrients, especially with today's high fat and high carb/low nutritional value meals, and not to mention, all the drug induced nutritional deficiencies, people these days experience.

Another great healthy lifestyle hack that I came across and is fairly easy to incorporate into any lifestyle and provides a whole array of benefits is intermittent fasting. Intermittent fasting is an eating pattern that cycles between periods of fasting and periods of eating. It includes daily time-restricted eating (such as 16:8, fasting for 16 hours and eating for 8 hours), alternate day fasting, and periodic fasting. Intermittent fasting is especially helpful when treating diabetic patients. As Dr. Jason Fung, an adult nephrology specialist explains, in terms of insulin production, hormones and the pancreas regulate metabolism, and weight loss/gain, are the primary influencers. Fasting allows for the pancreas to heal, reset and correct its own insulin production. His methods include intermittent, alternate day and extended fasting, in combination with either animal or vegan based ketogenic diet. The more I listened to him and the more I dug into what other doctors are finding on the benefits of intermittent fasting, the clearer it has become that this is definitely something that everyone at some point, in some shape or form, should incorporate into their lifestyle. However, one must always consult with their doctor first before making any significant or drastic changes to their diet, especially if they have any underlying health conditions or are taking any medications.

As faith would have it, just as I was learning more and more about nutrition, lifestyle hacks, and energy healing, my best friend and mentor, started her own functional medicine coaching practice for pharmacists, which I was eager to join. I am excited to learn more about what functional medicine entails and what I can use and start implementing it. Not just in my personal life, but also in my loved one's lives and into my current retail pharmacy practice. I continue to expand my knowledge of all the possibilities and resources I can use to help someone achieve optimum health. It might be as simple as a consultation on healthy bedtime habits for someone who has trouble sleeping. Or monitoring for common side effects or nutritional deficiencies from complex drug regimens. I feel my personal journey with this health and wellness company, and my functional medicine training, has given me a new perspective and an advantage in patient care overall. I am beyond grateful for this opportunity.

Writing this chapter has allowed me to reflect, and walk you through, my own unique STORRIE™ and personal discoveries I've found to be helpful in growing and improving myself. Over the past few years of bettering myself, not just as an individual, but as a healthcare professional, I have learned so much. I truly believe that for healing to take place, we need to address the root cause of disease, and most importantly to start with what matters most, our own mindset!

As I wrap up, I'll leave you with this quote said by many, with a slight variation, "The quality of your thoughts determines the quality of your life." I challenge you to start paying attention to your everyday thoughts that come up all the time. Are they positive or negative? Once you realize and consciously are made aware of these thoughts, you can start to turn some of the negative self-talk into thinking positive thoughts. Consistency is key, as with anything else in life. Your journey begins when you start making decisions that are in line with your goals, dreams, and passions and take consistent daily actions towards them. Doing so will, no doubt, start to manifest greatness into your quality of life. It's time to decide what your dream life looks like. It's time to commit to doing whatever it takes to make it happen. It's time to succeed and reap the benefits of your consistent actions by stepping into the life you CAN have!

ABOUT DR. ZSUZSANNA CONIGLIO

Dr. Zsuzsanna Coniglio, PharmD, is a Certified Functional Medicine Specialist™ from Functional Medicine Business Academy™ and Lifestyle Coach specializing in Integrative Pharmacy and Reiki Level I & II, as well as a loving mother of two. She is the founder and CEO of *Holistic Approach to Positive Inner-balance and Energy* (HAPIE). For the past 14 years, Dr. Zsuzsanna has been working as a retail pharmacist, with the majority of her time as a pharmacy manager at her community pharmacy. During these years, she has gained invaluable experience in pharmacy management and patient care, while collaborating with doctors and patients to achieve favorable outcomes in patients' health. She has always worked with the intention of building trust along the way.

In 2015, Dr. Zsuzsanna was given the unique opportunity to be part of a health and wellness company which opened her eyes to holistic living and the benefits of a healthy lifestyle. On this new journey she experienced an amazing health transformation, not just in herself, but more amazingly in her teenage son who looked up to her as his role model. This experience inspired her to learn all she can about healthy mindset, nutrition, holistic living, which all led her to pursue her functional medicine practitioner certification.

Dr. Zsuzsanna helps her clients to identify the "root cause" of their symptoms while giving them the tools and assisting them in taking charge of their health. She has developed a life-changing method for her clients by helping them implement a personalized plan using holistic medicine and practices that create desirable results and lead to an improved quality of life for each individual.

www.drzsuzsannaconiglio.com | drzsuzsannaconiglio@gmail.com

Made in the USA
Monee, IL
27 February 2022